YOUNG BLOOD

YOUNG BLOOD

the story of the family murders

BOB O'BRIEN

HarperCollins*Publishers*

HarperCollins*Publishers*

First published in Australia in 2002
by HarperCollins*Publishers* Australia Pty Limited
ABN 36 009 913 517
A member of the HarperCollins*Publishers* (Australia) Pty Limited Group
www.harpercollins.com.au

HarperCollins*Publishers*
25 Ryde Road, Pymble, Sydney, NSW 2073, Australia
31 View Road, Glenfield, Auckland 10, New Zealand
77–85 Fulham Palace Road, London W6 8JB, United Kingdom
2 Bloor Street East, 20th floor, Toronto, Ontario M4W 1A8, Canada
10 East 53rd Street, New York, NY 10022, USA

National Library of Australia Cataloguing-in-Publication data:

O'Brien, Bob, 1949– .
Young blood: the story of the family murders.
ISBN 978-0-7322-6913-5.
1. Einem, Bevan Spencer von. 2. Kelvin, Richard.
3. Murder – South Australia – Adelaide.
4. Murderers – South Australia – Adelaide.
I. Title.
364.15230994231

Cover and internal design by Luke Causby, HarperCollins Design Studio
Cover and spine photographs used courtesy of the *Advertiser*
Typeset in 10.5/16 Sabon by HarperCollins Design Studio

To Trevor Kipling
and dedicated professionals
within the Criminal Justice System

Contents

Acknowledgments

Many people assisted with the telling of this story. In particular, I thank Lee Haddon, Malcolm Howells, Tony Love, Jodie O'Brien, Des Phillips, Ivan Sarvas and Lois Snow for their encouragement and support.

Also, I acknowledge the work of M.L. Dietz, J. Douglas, J. Norris and M. Olshaker, which provided much of the detail about serial killers in Chapter 5.

Introduction

Adelaide is no different from any other city when it comes to crime. It has its traffic offenders, its petty thieves, its drug users and dealers and its murderers. But somehow Adelaide has earned a reputation for having more than its fair share of killers — and weird, sick ones at that.

That reputation has been earned by the city in spite of itself. Adelaide has always had a sense of difference about it. When it was established in the late 1830s the city was well planned: a square mile encased by a ring of parklands, with fine city parks in each of its quarters and a main central square that took the name of Victoria, Queen of England. A small river, the Torrens, created a green corridor just to the north of the main city area, separating it from another small section, North Adelaide, built on a rise and populated by the colony's wealthiest residents. Adelaide was different, too, because while most of Australia's cities began their histories as penal colonies, South Australia was a province of free settlers.

This heritage remained a touchstone, the city forging a name for its culture, its charm and its lifestyle. It is home to a world famous Festival of Arts. Its wide streets and historic buildings impart a sense of space and calm compared to the rush and bustle of many of Australia's larger capitals, and its lifestyle revolves around a social charm that has come from a Mediterranean climate coupled with a focus on excellent food and wine. This is seemingly intensified by Adelaide's place in the South Australian landscape. The city is hemmed in by successive arcs of low mountain ranges, wine growing areas and, finally, the harsh and unforgiving Outback.

With such a history and setting, Adelaide has always been thought of as a large country town. A nice place to live. The strength of its society, with great landed interests and moral obligations, built another reputation — Adelaide became known as the 'City of Churches'.

But beneath all of these conservative and wealthy trappings, people's lives in its expanding suburbs had all the complications experienced elsewhere. Every city has its underbelly and Adelaide was no different in that sense. In fact, author Salman Rushdie once declared after a visit to its arts festival that Adelaide was the 'perfect setting for a ... horror film', and that 'sleepy conservative towns are where those things happen'.

It is the horror of many of Adelaide's strange murders that nowadays peppers its international name. Why, in the second half of the 20th century, did a whole string of abductions and killings target such a nice community's children, adolescents and young adults? Why have many of these remained unsolved, leaving a bitter taste of unfinished business in the mouths of families and law agencies?

Some of these murders were no doubt single acts of madness. But some were so incomprehensibly deliberate and so heartless the psyche of the city was damaged forever. Why, people now ask, is Adelaide the home of Australia's weirdest killers?

Unfortunately, the catalogue of murders at the centre of these questions does not shed any light on an answer.

Three of them have baffled Adelaide's police force for close to thirty years. They remain unsolved, and detectives were powerless in a way because they simply didn't understand the killings. They didn't understand why they occurred or what sort of person would commit them.

Firstly, in 1966, three young children disappeared from the city's most popular beach, Glenelg. It was Australia Day and nothing more un-Australian could have been imagined. The three children from one family, the Beaumonts, were thought to have been abducted, and after extensive searching, and many publicly shocking leads, they were never found and were presumed murdered. What remains from the case is that name — the Beaumont children — which has stuck in the minds of all South Australians as a catchphrase for the day the nicest city in Australia lost its innocence. What also remains for many is the image of an eerie identikit illustration of a thin, harmless looking man, perhaps in his 20s or 30s, who was seen lurking in the area at the time. Whatever became of him? Was he indeed the sick criminal responsible? We will never know.

Seven years later, the disappearance of two young girls from an Aussie Rules football match at the picturesque Adelaide Oval, situated on the banks of the Torrens River just a kilometre from the city's central business district, was equally troublesome. The oval was packed with people watching their favourite winter sport when the two girls, Joanne Ratcliffe, eleven, and friend Kirsty Gordon, four, left their parents to go to a toilet within the grounds. In any proper society there shouldn't have been a problem. The toilets were not far away, the place was crowded with similar family folk — but the two girls were never seen again.

The person responsible was never found, and all the bad memories surrounding the case of the Beaumont children came flooding back into the minds of South Australians. The places where they had always felt at home, always felt secure, where they went to enjoy their free time at the beach or at the footy, were no longer safe. More importantly, their children were no longer safe. The quiet, peaceful life they had always known had taken a turn for the worse, and the question on many lips was whether the same evil mind was responsible for both shocking crimes. Again, the police could give the public no solution to allay their fears.

Another child's abduction in 1982 brought all these thoughts back into focus just as Adelaide's memory of these unusual crimes was beginning to fade. This time young Louise Bell was abducted while she slept in her own home in the southern suburbs. A stranger entered her bedroom through the window and walked out the front door with the small child, neither ever to be seen again. Louise's mother was asleep in the house at the time. How could such a heinous crime occur? Who on earth would do such a thing? Was nothing, not even our own homes, sacred anymore?

The fear in people's minds undoubtedly was that out there, somewhere in Adelaide's suburbs, a killer or killers preying on the community's children was still on the loose — and police had been unable to track them down.

There had been other murders, however, which had been easier to solve. One, in particular, in 1971, was a tragic crime of passion, a multiple killing spree unleashed by Clifford Bartholomew against his family at Hope Forest, south of Adelaide. In the end Bartholomew's wife and nine children, from the baby to the teenagers, had been shot dead, and he had been dealt with by the police and convicted by the court.

In the scheme of things, this was like many multiple killings elsewhere in the world. A mad moment in which all hell breaks loose and a man, usually a husband, murders his wife and children. In policing terms the crime is easily identifiable. The person who 'loses the plot' is usually found nearby and the legal system does its work, for right or wrong. The family is devastated and the community's collective heart goes out to all those concerned.

In Adelaide, the Hope Forest murders served to highlight the difference between such an explosive, one-off event, and the still unsolved, gradually unfolding series of abductions and presumed killings that haunted the state's psyche over the next two decades. Was there a cold and calculating serial killer still prowling the city and, if so, where would his deliberations lead him next?

The answer to that question took an unfortunate twist in the summer of 1976–77 when seven young women, aged from their mid-teens to mid-twenties, were snatched from Adelaide's city centre and northern suburbs in just a few months. The bodies weren't found for more than a year: the first of them, that of Veronica Knight, by a mushroomer in April, 1978, in harsh, dry scrubland near a township called Truro, about 100 kilometres north of Adelaide. In the end five of the girls were found in the area, dumped haphazardly under shrubs and fallen trees, some not even buried. Although the other victims were found elsewhere, the unfolding saga soon became known as the 'Truro murders'.

Once again the police were under increasing pressure to rid the city of a menace that had invaded its quiet streets. Glen Lawrie and Peter Foster were the two detectives from Major Crime working on the case when they received what police call 'information from the public', another term for one person dobbing in another. Someone out there obviously had a guilty conscience, or was seeking revenge, perhaps a reward. Maybe someone with a strong moral sense was just trying to do the right thing.

Whatever the reason, the information helped solve the case and led the detectives to uncover that Christopher Worrell, a good-looking, young bisexual who had 'form', and his current boyfriend, James Miller, had been picking up the young women, driving them to remote locations and killing them. It seemed a careless and crazy series of events; the official reason that was given was that Worrell killed the girls because he had been in jail before for attempting to rape a female and he did not want to go back in again.

The real reason for the murder spree, no doubt, was that he perhaps lost control the first time, then realised he enjoyed it. Miller, who at the time was totally infatuated with Worrell, acted as the driver. Although police could not prove that Miller actually killed any of the girls, he knew what Worrell was doing, he actively assisted him and so, as an accomplice, he was found guilty of murder.

There was an unusual turn in the case, however, which strangely affected the community's sense of closure of the shocking series of events. Worrell had been killed in a car accident just days after the final young woman had been murdered in February 1977. It was this simple twist of fate that stopped the killings.

There was a second twist in the Truro serial murders that seemed even more bizarre. There was a sexual deviation at play here that for many was incomprehensible. The City of Churches was having to come to grips with what once was a nice, conservative life unravelling before its very eyes. Babies snatched from their bedrooms, young children disappearing from their favourite haunts, now killers unleashing a torrent of violence against the weaker sex.

It was all too weird, but what was about to happen over the next few years changed Adelaide's reputation once and for all. For even as the police were solving the case of the Truro murders, another bout of serial killings was already underway. This time it was the turn of young men to be snatched from the city's streets, and this time the investigation was to reveal what were perhaps some of the most shocking details ever uncovered about the way the mind of a serial killer works. In the process another dark chapter in Adelaide's criminal record was opened.

This case would eventually become known as the 'Family Murders', implicating, rightly or wrongly, members of the elite of South Australian society. But what kind of 'family' would act like this? And what kind of community could continue to tolerate such an intrusion upon their lives? Strangely nothing about the murders leading up to this point seemed to intersect. Would this be the case that might answer some of the questions now being asked about the bizarre killers lurking beneath the surface of one of Australia's nicest cities?

Chapter 1

The Butchered Boys

The young man's body should have disappeared below the cold, grey-brown waters of the South Para Reservoir, except the winter rains had not come in sufficient quantity to fill it. The water level was still low after Adelaide's hot summer, causing the old road and bridge to be exposed. The reservoir fits into the contours of the Adelaide Hills to the north-east of the city, the curves of the hills forcing the water into little valleys and taking the shape of a serpent's tail stretching out to the east where it is crossed by a new bridge that helps link the small hills communities of Williamstown and Kersbrook.

The cracked and unused road snakes down the hill towards the reservoir and flattens on the top of the old bridge that crosses the South Para Creek before climbing between the gum trees on the opposite side. The new bridge sits ten metres above the old road and bridge and is much longer, as it spans the 100-metre gap between the hills. If you stop in the middle of it you might think that you would be stopping over water but the ramp running to the northern side of the old bridge is immediately below.

Alan Barnes was dropped over the side of the new bridge, discarded like an uncaring person would discard a bag of rubbish. His back broke when it hit the hard mud but he did not feel his bones break. His ability to feel pain had left him long before he was thrown over the tubular rails of the bridge. Before he was dumped he had been harmed beyond any hope of recovery — his anus was split open, allowing his blood to pour from his body. Once the tearing started, shock set in and his body gave up its fight to live. The pain, alcohol and drugs that he had been given prevented much of a struggle. He died before half an hour had passed.

Alan disappeared on Sunday 17 June 1979. He was found exactly a week later when a bush walker and his girlfriend parked their motorcycle and climbed over the fence and entered the grounds of the reservoir. They walked down the old road and saw the body of Alan Barnes. He had landed on the earth that ran alongside the old road and not into the waters of the reservoir as most likely had been intended. If Alan Barnes had landed in the water and descended to the mud on the bottom of the reservoir he would never have been found. He would have remained another missing person.

The deviates who had murdered the boy had made their first mistake.

Alan Barnes was a product of Salisbury, a suburb sitting on the hot flat plains about twenty kilometres north of central Adelaide. Salisbury grew as migrants from England and the rest of Europe moved to the open spaces where there were opportunities for jobs and houses of their own. The immigrants were promised a cheap passage to Australia and a new life.

Alan was the first of a new generation of Australians born and bred in our changing world. He was young and experimenting with life, with all the hope of a promising future ahead of him. His blond hair and good looks ensured that he always had company to enjoy life with but with them came the opportunities to experiment with drugs that had become freely available in Adelaide in the 1970s. He had stayed overnight with a friend in a house in the north-western suburb of Cheltenham. Alan and his friend woke about mid-day and ate a meal of fried eggs on toast before being driven to Grand Junction Road and left to hitchhike to Alan's home in Salisbury. The two young men were not having much success getting a lift so his friend headed home, thinking Alan would have a better chance to get a lift by himself. Alan was last seen trying his luck getting home on Grand Junction Road.

His mother, Judy, reported him missing to the police the next day, when he had not come home. Police appeals for people who may have seen him produced few results even though he was on a main arterial road within a city of one million people. One caller to police thought that he had seen Alan getting into a car on Grand Junction Road. The car was described as a white Holden sedan with three or four people in it.

A week later, local officers greeted the detectives from the Major Crime Squad on the dirt verge on the northern side of the South Para Bridge. They moved down the slope to view Alan's body. The detectives waited for the police photographers to arrive to record the location and body, and for crime scene examiners to scour the location for any evidence. Some stood with their hands in their pockets looking at the body from about ten metres away. They distanced themselves from the body to make sure that their footprints were not disturbing any footprints or evidence around the body. They stood with their hands in their pockets because they had been trained to do so. Leaving their hands in their pockets made sure they didn't touch murder weapons or items left at the scene of a crime. The sort of cop show scenario where detectives pick up a gun by putting a biro in the end of its barrel only happens on television. Police officers who are crime scene examiners doing that sort of work day in and day out don't place biros into gun barrels. However, they need not have worried, as the only evidence was the body of Alan Barnes — and the abnormal twist in his body indicated that he had been dropped from the bridge. A search of the bridge revealed nothing of interest on the concrete and tar.

After the police crime scene examiners and photographers finished, the coroner's staff placed Alan in a body bag and zipped it up. They placed him in a plain white van. He was driven to the Forensic Science Centre in Divett Place, Adelaide, where the van's driver signalled the security officer to raise the roller door at the rear of the building. Alan Barnes was taken from the van and placed onto one of the three mortuary slabs in the rear of the building. Pathologist Dr Colin Manock carried out the post-mortem examination of the lad. He assessed the injury as mostly likely to have been caused by an object similar to a bottle with a tapered neck being inserted into Alan's anus so far that it caused tearing of the skin and opening of the blood vessels. The injuries caused massive bleeding. There was a catch, however. When the boy was found he was fully clothed and no blood had soaked into the fabric of his clothes. The only marks on the clothes were from the reservoir mud.

It was not unusual for young men to go missing. It is not unusual for young men to be murdered. What was unusual was the mutilation of this body. Death from ruptured tissues surrounding the anus was unusual. Alan Barnes had been undressed and abused — that too was unusual. Usually, when a person is abused, killed and dumped, it's a woman. This time it was a young man.

Unfortunately, detectives made little progress toward solving the murder of Alan Barnes. Police received some tip offs but no solid evidence was forthcoming. As well, Major Crime detectives were busy finishing paper work after investigating the serial killings of seven young women that had become known as the Truro murders. This case had just 'burst wide open' when James William Miller was charged with the Truro murders just one month before Alan Barnes was found. The media largely forgot the Alan Barnes murder — there were too many front-page stories about Truro for reporters to be writing stories about Alan Barnes. Besides, there were no leaks from the police that indicated that they were close to solving this new murder. The leads being followed by detectives were not going anywhere.

When the mutilated body of Neil Frederick Muir was found on Tuesday 28 August 1979, the media did not report a connection between the two murders. Two months had passed since the murder of Alan Barnes and the disposal of Neil Muir did not indicate killings committed by the same people — not in the beginning, anyway.

This murder was even more bizarre. Neil's body was found floating in shallow water of the Port River, a tidal estuary joining the sea at the top of Le Fevre Peninsular, which runs north and south for about twelve kilometres and is shaped like a small thumb extending from the Adelaide Plains. Ground water feeds into the estuary from the wealthy suburb of West Lakes, which was designed and built on small, undulating sandhills and low-lying land that absorbed the water flowing from the Adelaide hills onto the plains.

As with Alan Barnes, it had been intended that Neil Muir would disappear under the surface of the water, never to be seen again. He was dropped from the wharf built at the end of Veitch Road, near the top of the peninsular. The remote and disused wharf serviced Mutton Cove on the eastern side of the Port River. The dock is no longer used, except by line fishermen trying to catch bream and other small fish in the river.

Neil Muir was not just killed and thrown off the wharf. He was stuffed into a plastic garbage bag. To make him fit into the bag, his head and his legs were cut off, his intestines removed and his legs shoved inside his carcass. The head was tied to the torso with yellow plastic cord, which passed up through the severed neck and back through the mouth and looped through the top ribs. The resulting sight was bizarre. Neil's head was attached to his body by cord rather than by his neck.

His feet stuck out of his carcass but the body was now small enough to fit in the bag, which was then wrapped with cord to hold everything together. When the whole package had been thrown into the river at Mutton Cove, the murderers had not realised that the tidal flow of the river leaves the bottom of mud and rocks exposed at low tide. The bag jagged on the partially exposed rocks and a local worker with the Department of Marine and Harbours found the gruesome container. The worker was planning to go fishing at the Cove — but that day he found more than bream.

Mutton Cove, I thought cynically. *What an appropriate name to find such a carcass.*

An *Advertiser* reporter and photographer were present when the police divers lifted the body bag up onto the wharf, so the media knew that Neil Muir had been cut up. But they didn't know the full extent of his injuries. Pathologist Dr Ross James revealed the additional injuries when he examined Neil Muir's remains on the same mortuary slab where Alan Barnes was placed just over two months previously.

Neil Muir received a blow to the head shortly before his death but the whack did not kill him. The post-mortem examination revealed the cause of death. Neil Muir, like Alan Barnes, also had horrible injuries to his anus. Neil's anus had also been torn by the insertion of something like the neck of a tapered bottle, which had been inserted so far that the skin could not stretch any further. As the bottle-like object was forced upward even further, the skin ripped apart, rupturing blood vessels and causing massive bleeding. The blood loss and shock from the tearing caused Neil Muir to die.

After he was killed, a saw had been used to cut his spine in two places. His head had been sawn off at the neck. His arms and legs were neatly cut from his body at the joints. The lower arms and legs had been cut from the upper arms and legs. All fingers and thumbs had been cut off and his pelvis had been separated from his torso and backbone. The teeth marks from the saw could be seen on the C 4 vertebra where the head had been cut from the body. The same saw marks could be seen on L 4 of the spine, where the pelvic bones had been separated from the torso.

As well as being dissected, Neil Muir's flesh and muscle tissue had been removed from his arms and upper legs, leaving bare bones. All internal organs — the heart, lungs, liver, kidney and intestines — had been removed. His scrotum had been cut open and his testicles had been removed. The head of his penis had been cut off and his penis shaft had been cut open down the middle. One testicle was missing. Neil Muir's tattoos were cut from his arms and legs and placed in a separate plastic bag and placed inside his torso along with his arms and legs.

The cutting up of the body was gruesome but, in this sordid case, understandable. Murderers trying to get rid of a corpse might consider making it as small as possible for carting around and also easier to dump. It was the other injuries that were harder to understand. The removal of fingers and tattoos could have been a bungled attempt to prevent the police finding the identity of the body in the bag. However, when the pathologist found one testicle was missing, a new dimension to the case was presented to police. The person who removed that testicle did not do it to help dispose of Neil Muir or to stop police identifying the body. There had to be a more bizarre reason. Was it eaten in a bizarre ritual or was it kept as a hideous souvenir, in the manner of some serial killers? These were the kind of questions going through police minds at the time.

This information was not released to the media, but detectives were worried. Neil Muir was a known drugs user, and later they learned Alan Barnes had been starting to use marijuana and other drugs. Neil had passed the experimental stage with drugs. He was addicted to heroin and was participating in a methadone trial at Hillcrest Hospital in the north-eastern suburbs. Neil Muir, like Alan Barnes, was relatively good looking and even though Neil Muir was older than Alan Barnes — Neil was twenty-five and Alan was sixteen — both were too young to die, especially to be killed in a way that was so depraved and brutal. The anal injuries to both of the young men were bad enough, but the dissection of Neil Muir was so barbarous that it even stopped the cynical humour of hardened detectives. They became increasingly concerned, as the dumping into water was similar to that of Alan Barnes and the anal injuries were also similar. Two young men killed in the same way within two months of one another started speculation that a serial killer was at work on the streets of the city. The second murder caused increased pressure on detectives attached to the Major Crime Squad.

Detectives from the Major Crime Squad continued investigating leads but as time passed the intensity of inquiries lessened as public concern about the murders dissipated. Detectives went back to investigating crimes of passion — murders that occur when people who know each other become frustrated and angry — angry enough for one to kill the other. A mate kills a mate. A husband kills his wife.

Then, two years after Neil Muir, another young man, Mark Andrew Langley, went missing.

Renewed vigour, and not a little tension returned to the Major Crime Squad when, in March 1982, Langley's mutilated body was found in the Adelaide Hills. Mark had the same type of anal injury as Alan Barnes and Neil Muir.

Mark Langley had been driving in the city with two friends when they decided to stop on War Memorial Drive, which curves and bends following the northern bank of the River Torrens. It was late at night. The warm Saturday evening was typical for Adelaide. They had left a party and the three of them wanted to go to the city. Mark's friend Ian Samson drove into War Memorial Drive and angle-parked his white Datsun 1600 on the northern side of the road. The Saturday night had moved to Sunday morning and at 1.30 a.m. the area was dark and quiet.

War Memorial Drive cuts through parklands that separate the CBD from North Adelaide. During the day the road is used by commuters for parking before they cross the river to go to their offices in the city. Students also park and cross the footbridge linking the two roads on either side of the river to go to lectures at the University of Adelaide. Very early in the morning and on weekends rowers use the road to get to the boatsheds scattered along the banks of the river. The road is not used much at night, except to provide car parking for people going to shows in the city or by lovers stopping under the trees later in the night.

A large gum tree separated their car from the Adelaide University Boat Club building that stood to their right, its branches sheltering the car from the light falling from the few streetlights in the drive. The playing grounds of the university football club spread out in front of their car. The three of them: Mark, Ian and Ian's girlfriend, Paula, were sitting in their car when an argument started between Mark and Ian. They argued over some cigarettes, but whether the argument had really happened because of that, or competition between the two young men over the single girl, is not clear. Two young males sitting with a pretty girl late at night is a potentially explosive mix.

Mark Langley did not like the way the argument was going. He got out of the car, fuming over the way things had gone. Mark walked into the blackness of the night.

The argument indicated a lack of maturity that was not evident in his manly physical appearance. Mark Langley was tall, strong and good-looking. Thick tufts of chest hair protruded from the open shirts that he wore. His black chest hair contrasted with the silver chain and the ingot engraved with the crab, his Cancer star sign, which he wore around his neck.

Ian Sampson and Paula Atkinson initially drove off, circling and driving over the bridge near the Adelaide Zoo past the University on their left and Jolly's Boathouse on their right before turning onto the King William Street

Bridge and returning to their parking spot. They were gone for about four minutes. Mark had not returned. They drove around trying to find him but he had disappeared.

Mark's family worriedly contacted friends and relatives over the remainder of the weekend but no one had seen or heard from Mark. As their concern heightened, they rang the police on Sunday evening to report him missing.

Police filled out a missing person's report and circulated the information; but their question was simply 'Where do you start looking?' The young man disappeared within a large city. There are no easy answers when investigating reports of missing people. Information is needed and that information was presented to police nine days later, on March 8.

A local Adelaide Hills dweller was poisoning blackberry bushes on the side of Sprigg Road, Summertown, which nestles on the rear slopes of Mount Lofty close to three high-powered television towers that dominate the city skyline from the southern ridge leading to the Mount Lofty summit. The hills formed a barrier to the growth of the city of Adelaide, forcing it to spread north and south along the Adelaide plains, trapped between the waters of the Gulf of St Vincent and the grey-green hills to the east. The local, moving through the grass and bushes, found Mark lying on the ground close to the road, partly concealed by the scrubby landscape. He was dressed but his skull and neck were exposed and the hot weather had started to putrefy the exposed parts of his body. Blue jeans still protected his lower body.

Mark Langley had also been redressed and placed into the clothes that he was wearing the night he disappeared. He had been wearing a blue woollen cardigan, a smart blue satin shirt to match his blue jeans, and that distinctive chain with his Cancer star sign on a silver ingot. Mark was still wearing the same clothes but his necklace and shirt were missing. At some stage his shirt had been removed and his cardigan put back on. While the forensic examination at Divett Place revealed other injuries that were similar to those inflicted on Alan Barnes and Neil Muir, there was something different this time. Mark Langley had suffered the same tearing to his anus, but there was a wound to his abdomen that had been stitched up — he had been operated on, sewn up and then reclothed.

The cut in the abdomen started about five centimetres above the penis and travelled vertically towards the navel. The incision was 16.5 centimetres long and slightly to the right of the middle of his abdomen. The body hair around the wound had been shaved and the incision had been stitched together with a three-ply polyester filament before being taped over with a Johnson & Johnson type surgical tape.

Mark Langley also had anal injuries similar to Alan Barnes and Neil Muir. Police wondered whether or not the same people were involved and if there were other boys missing that they did not know about.

In fact, there was another body waiting to be found. Peter Stogneff had been abducted twelve months after the dissection of Neil Muir but his body was not found until after Mark Langley had been killed.

Peter Stogneff also lived in one of the northern suburbs of Adelaide. His home was the normal dwelling of a middle-class family in one of the newer suburbs of Adelaide. He wagged school on Thursday, 27 August 1981, six months before Mark Langley disappeared.

Like the others, Peter's family reported him missing that evening and media coverage failed to attract any response in finding him.

Peter was the youngest of the boys. He was fourteen. Alan Barnes was sixteen, Neil Muir twenty-five and Mark Langley nineteen when they went missing. Peter was, like the others, young, and good looking. Friends knew that he was going to wag school. He left his home first thing in the morning carrying his school bag, and his parents were none the wiser about his plans for the day. Peter returned home later that morning, possibly after going off to the Tea Tree Plaza, a local shopping centre, where kids congregate. He left his school bag in the garage and then left again, heading for the city to meet his friend Daniel Tzeganoff at the silver balls sculpture in Rundle Mall, which runs off King William Street. Peter Stogneff did not meet his mate; he, too, just disappeared.

Ten months later, on 23 June 1982, his remains were found on the side of Middle Beach Road, Two Wells. Middle Beach is about twenty kilometres north of Le Fevre Peninsular and is best known for the shacks that shelter the holiday makers who like to walk out in the low tidal waters to catch blue crabs. A local farmer had cleared grass and bushes on the side of the dirt road near his farm, pushing the unwanted material into piles to allow them to dry before setting fire to them some months later when the weather was cooler. Now, in winter, he followed through with his plans, and was checking the remains of the fires several days later when he found the burnt skeleton. Detectives believed that they were the boy's remains but identification was difficult. Only the skeleton remained and no clothes or personal effects were found amongst the debris. This time pathologist Dr Derreck Pounder examined the remains. The size and shape of the skull and examination of the teeth caused the coroner to later conclude that it was Peter Stogneff.

Like Neil Muir, Peter had been cut up with a saw. His back had been sawn through leaving an oblique cut. The legs had been cut above the knees with the same saw and his lower legs were missing. The people who were killing these boys now were not even trying to dispose of the bodies. The first and second were dumped into water with the expectation that they would be lost out of sight but Mark Langley was dumped alongside a dirt road not far from Mount Lofty, the highest point of the Adelaide Hills, which overlooks the city. Now, Peter Stogneff had been dumped on the side of a nearby country road.

South Australia now had four young men killed in a relatively short space of time. Three had anal injuries, so it was possible that the same people killed three of them — Barnes, Muir and Langley. The fourth, Peter Stogneff, was cut up — not exactly in the same way as Neil Muir but similarly enough to make detectives wonder whether or not the same people killed them. If the same people killed Muir and Stogneff, then perhaps the same people had killed them all.

Those questions were now in the minds of the police when another young man disappeared. This time the public's attention skyrocketed.

❂ ❂ ❂

Richard Kelvin lived with his mum and dad in North Adelaide amongst some of the smartest houses of the city. Rob and Betteanne Kelvin lived in a modern townhouse in one of the newer developments of the time. Their home was 'trendy' but Rob and Betteanne were down to earth people who did not exude airs and graces. Their modern comfortable home stood about one kilometre from the Torrens River and less than half that distance from O'Connell Street, the main shopping road of North Adelaide, which splits North Adelaide into two. The broad street allows traffic from the CBD to pass through the northern suburbs before heading to the premier wine district, the Barossa Valley.

Rob was working for Channel Nine, the local television station that consistently won the ratings war against the three other local television stations. Channel Nine started broadcasting television to excited South Australians before any of the other rivals and the station has never looked back. Rob Kelvin joined Channel Nine after working as a journalist on Adelaide radio. He was well known from radio and his profile had become higher presenting the news-bulletin.

Rob and his two boys were playing at home on the weekend. It was 5–6 June 1983. Richard played football for a Lockleys football club on the Saturday and Rob had been kicking the football with his eldest son, Richard, at one of the nearby parks on Sunday. Richard's best mate Karl 'Boris' Brooks was with them. Richard was a normal fifteen-year-old Australian boy. He was tall for his age, good looking and had blond hair. He liked sport, he put up with school and had just found a girlfriend.

He met his girlfriend at the Prospect Oval, a football ground where the North Adelaide football team play. They had been going together for over a month. She was similar in age and height, she was pretty and he really liked her. He liked having a girlfriend. They rang each other just about every day and went to the movies together. They even talked about getting engaged in four years time when they would be nineteen. Richard and Boris were speaking to the girl on the phone just before they walked to O'Connell Street. He said that he'd ring her back after he walked with Boris to the bus stop.

Richard and Boris walked along Ward Street, turned right onto O'Connell Street and stopped next to the yellow bus stop in front of a delicatessen. Although it was Sunday and some of the shops were closed, O'Connell Street was still active, with cars passing by and people walking to the restaurants and cafes across the road. A grey government bus arrived a few minutes after they walked to the bus stop. Frank Marrollo got off with his cousin, Frank D'Antiocchia. Marrollo spoke to Richard, who he knew as 'Sticks' while Boris got onto the bus. The three boys knew each other and spoke as Boris stepped onto the bus to ride home. Everything was still OK. Richard started to head home, about 400 metres away, to have dinner with his parents and younger brother.

But Richard Kelvin didn't arrive home. Like the other boys before him, he simply disappeared. None of the neighbours saw him that afternoon. They did not see him walk to the bus stop nor did they see him walk home. No-one saw him arrive home because he never made it.

Chapter 2

The Search for Richard Kelvin

I had just moved to the Major Crime Squad when the remains of Peter Stogneff were found near Middle Beach. Detectives from the squad were already working on the Alan Barnes, Neil Muir and Mark Langley cases.

Major Crime investigates crimes that are too difficult or protracted for detectives posted in the suburbs. The squad's main job is investigating murders, while a small group within the squad deals with armed robberies. However, any crime that is serious and causes community concern can be handled by the squad, which is made up of small teams led by a Senior Sergeant supported by two sergeants and four detectives. The two sergeants are senior investigators rather than supervisors.

I was pleased and excited to join the team led by Glen Lawrie who previously had teamed with Peter Foster and become well known as the detective who got James Miller to confess to his involvement in the Truro murders. Glen was relatively young to be a senior sergeant but he was smart and his success in solving the Truro murders would have helped him get his promotion. He was tall and fit — he liked to ride his pushbike home in the Adelaide Hills on occasions and with his fitness and long, shoulder-length hair he did not conform to the image of some older style, hard-drinking detectives in the squad.

I admit I was relatively young and ambitious. I'd wanted to be a police officer for as long as I could remember. Dad was a police officer and I wanted to do the same things that he did. I'd moved through the police ranks after graduating second from Fort Largs police academy.

Like all new graduates, I'd walked beats before being allowed to ride in patrol cars with the more experienced officers. My first brief as a police officer happened when I reported a driver for displaying an expired registration disc on his motor car. Hardly a capital crime! But over the years I learnt the trick to being a policeman. I transferred from Adelaide patrols to the traffic branch and rode motorcycles for five years. The work was a bit boring but I loved riding the bikes — I learned to ride police motorcycles because in the old days it was a stepping stone to detective work. Police motorcyclists rode alone and without radio communications in those years. You learned to be self-reliant and able to operate alone.

My first detective posting was at Holden Hill Criminal Investigation Branch in the northern suburbs of Adelaide. I worked there for a couple of months before being transferred to the detective office at Elizabeth. The districts around Elizabeth consisted of lower socio-economic groups among whom crime was a part of life. I learned the art of investigation, and my experience was given a great boost when I was sent back to headquarters to help with the Truro murders. As a very junior detective, it was exciting to see the Major Crime Squad buzzing with a major murder case on its hands.

I spent about six months in the squad taking statements and following up minor bits of information about the Truro killings. During my time there Alan Barnes was killed, but I was too engrossed with Truro to hear much scuttlebutt about his murder. Detectives working on cases generally keep the details close to their chests to prevent sensitive information being leaked. It's important that detectives withhold certain bits of information. Occasionally, 'nutters' will confess to a crime even though they didn't do it. If certain bits of information are kept in-house then detectives can tell whether or not a person is actually telling the truth. A person confessing to killing someone and saying they have tied the victim with rope when wire was used signals to detectives that something is wrong.

I returned to the Elizabeth detective office just before Neil Muir's dismembered body was found in the Port River.

After Elizabeth, I spent a bit of time helping out in the Drug Squad but I wanted to have a go at investigating murders. My appetite was whetted after my secondment to Major Crime and I requested a posting to the squad. When I was transferred there in 1982, one of the sergeants on Glen Lawrie's team was a senior detective called Trevor Kipling. I called him 'Kippers', not only because of his surname but because he liked fishing. He was already working on the Mark Langley case. I had first met Trevor when I spent my first months as a junior detective at Holden Hill. Trevor was a detective in the older style — he liked a drink and had a good sense of humour that brought out his strong belly laugh. He was tall, slightly taller than me, and his black hair had started to grey, complementing his blue eyes, which flashed when speaking to an attractive woman but turned a steel colour when his determination to prove a point came to the fore. Trevor was not university educated like many newer detectives but his high intelligence showed many times in the next few years.

Up to this time different teams were investigating the murder of the boys. The team that was working at the time a body was found usually ended up investigating the murder. Now it was different. There was a growing realisation that the murders of the young men could be linked. Bodies with anal injuries. Bodies being cut up. There were too many similarities to be ignored. The realisation was like a mudslide building into an avalanche. Police inside Major Crime talked more and more about the multiples of missing young men.

To combine the investigations, the team investigating the missing boys came to Senior Sergeant Glen Lawrie's team.

He'd been on a bit of a roll after solving the Truro murders, and while many people had been involved, it was Lawrie who'd managed to get James Miller to talk and take the police to the girls' bodies that had not been found. Now, Glen Lawrie was about to turn his attention to the series of murdered boys.

Glen was introducing me to the day-to-day work of Major Crime. I went with him to the flat farming land to the north of the city, where Peter Stogneff was dropped alongside the dirt road between the fence line and straight edge of the road. The area was featureless and it would have been very easy for a car to stop and empty its boot of Peter's body and abandon it amongst the bushes. Nobody was near enough to notice. Visiting the locations where bodies were dumped allowed me to get a feel for the type of person who was doing these murders. Obviously, a car had to be used and either the person had to be strong enough to lift a body or more than one person was involved.

Within a very short time I was investigating murders and then assisting with the Kelvin disappearance. At the time, I didn't realise just how much I would become involved and how it would become part of my life.

I had a professional relationship with the Kelvins. I never became as close to them as a friend but I liked the family. Rob Kelvin had a high profile, and he was popular — but he seemed a genuinely nice guy. He was the same in real life as he appeared on television. He was competent and professional without any big headedness. He was not snobbish, and because of that I liked the man. Rob was alarmed and worried about his son's disappearance but he handled it by maintaining his composure, as he appears to do every night on television. Obviously, he has a strong side. His time as a patrol officer in New Guinea when he was a younger man also shows strength.

Betteanne, his wife, was also stoic about their son's disappearance but you could see their relatively calm exteriors hid immense suffering. She worked in a small store in the city and matched Rob perfectly. Rob and Betteanne Kelvin were normal people but the only difference was that Rob worked in an industry that caused him to have a very high profile. The disappearance of their son caused even more observation of their lives in the years to come.

The disappearance of Richard Kelvin didn't cause too many alarm bells to go off at first. Jim Munro, an older detective in Major Crime, and a bit of a snappy dresser, said to me the day after Richard had gone missing:

'He's run off with his girlfriend. You wait and see. He'll turn up.'

Jim figured that Richard was just one of many young men who go missing all the time.

Here we had a young man who had recently found a girlfriend. He was growing up quickly. He could easily have run away from home just like many others.

Jim was an experienced detective but he hadn't visited the Kelvin house the previous night. He didn't speak to Richard's parents and hear what the young man's new girlfriend said when she was interviewed. This one was different.

Kids growing up do have worries and concerns. They may not be happy at home and they leave. Parents arguing all the time may upset a kid who might want to get out of the house, or parents may be seen to be coming down on the child so much that it causes the kid to leave home. Neither of these were the case with Richard Kelvin.

Police rely on differences to help explain what has happened when disappearances occur. When a young man runs away from home he might be missing, but often there are some indications where he may be — he doesn't disappear without trace. His family may not know where he is but his friends do. Runaways don't just disappear. They have to stay somewhere, usually with friends or acquaintances. They have to eat somewhere, usually at their local haunts. There are nearby pinball parlors. And fish and chip shops. There's always somewhere and someone who knows them — and messages get back to the family and police. That tells us that they are still alive. If young men disappear interstate, then they still have to survive. Often welfare agencies become involved, and they encourage the boys to ring home. If they are old enough to receive welfare payments, then there are records of those payments. Police check with the welfare agencies to see whether or not the missing people are receiving any money. The money trail tells the police and family that they are still alive.

With Richard Kelvin, nothing suggested that he would have run off. He was happy that weekend. Having a kick of the football with his father on the Saturday went well. There were no arguments. He got on well with his mother. Boris's visit on the Sunday went well; there were no arguments and when he saw him go at the bus stop, Richard was happy. The two guys who got off the bus at the time saw both of them in O'Connell Street and confirmed this. Richard was due home straight away for dinner and it was agreed that he would ring his girlfriend — besides it was another excuse to speak to her.

One of the uniform patrols from the city attended their home after the Kelvin's call for help. At first, they did not think much about it as it was a weekend and there was nothing exciting about a missing fifteen-year-old. They were more interested, however, when they found out that it was the son of Rob Kelvin, the newsreader. This meant the media could be involved.

We better do this properly, they thought.

Once the uniformed officers heard the story they knew the disappearance was different from that of a normal runaway.

Police also spoke to Richard's girlfriend that night. She was surprised that her new boyfriend had not returned home straight away. Everything was alright when she spoke to him earlier, on the phone, before Boris left the Kelvin home. She said they made small talk. Everything was fine and she enjoyed his friendship.

Boris jumped on after the grey government bus pulled up to the stop with a hiss from the airbrakes. He moved to the left-hand side of the bus and leaned out of the window as he left.

'Praise the lord,' Boris yelled.

'Hallelujah,' Richard yelled out, grinning and holding his arms. Frank Marrollo stood there and laughed. Boris and Richard were sending up the group of preachers that were across the road on the opposite footpath of O'Connell Street calling out about the Lord and handing out religious pamphlets.

Richard was tall and his body was starting to develop and become muscular. Boris described the clothes he was wearing: blue jeans and a navy blue T-shirt with Channel Nine television station logos on the front and back. The shoes he wore were trendy Adidas sneakers; however, the dog collar he was wearing around his neck was different. Boris saw him playing with the collar from the Kelvin dog when they were speaking to Richard's girlfriend on the telephone. He saw the chrome metal studs circling the leather band, which stood out against his friend's white skin when he put it around his neck. It was so different that Richard took it off when his mate stirred him about it at the bus stop. He said it looked stupid and gay. That's when it came off. Richard wanted to look manly, not gay.

Over the following days, Rob and Betteanne were quietly asked about their son's sexuality, and they insisted he was not gay. The question was also put to his friends as discretely as possible. There was nothing to suggest that he was homosexual or bisexual. I never asked Rob or Betteanne about the dog collar that he wore. It wasn't the right time to be asking parents the reason why their missing son wore particular items. I thought that it did not suit his age or appearance but young men do wear things to make them look older or tougher or both. The dog collar and the way Richard went missing were the first of many unusual aspects to the boy's disappearance.

The uniformed officers did all that they could that Sunday evening. They drove around North Adelaide and spoke to people in the shops near the bus stop. Nothing. They contacted Adelaide detectives and put out a KLOF message to other police patrols. KLOF is an acronym meaning to 'keep look out for'. They couldn't do any more. The disappearance was definitely a strange one.

When a crime occurs, there is normally a crime scene. An abandoned car, a body or a burnt house remains. Police place a cordon around the scene to preserve any evidence that might remain. Crime scene examiners look for things like fingerprints on smooth surfaces, a discarded shell from the bullet of a gun, some blood or clothing left behind. The difficulty with Richard Kelvin's disappearance was that there was no crime scene to isolate for police to scour for evidence. The last known place where Richard stood was on the footpath of O'Connell Street and then there was nothing. We knew he had not arrived home. The area between the bus stop and Richard's home was too large an area to seal off. That left door knocking.

Police knock on the doors of people living near the scene of a crime to discover whether or not the home-owners have seen or heard anything. So police organised a door knock to occur the following day. The police use standard forms that ask the names of the people living in the house, whether or not they have heard or seen anything unusual and they leave a calling card with a police contact number.

Uniformed officers from Adelaide patrols and detectives from the Adelaide C.I.B. met outside the Kelvin home the following day. They were briefed about their duties, then sent to different homes between the Kelvin home and O'Connell Street.

The door knock over the next days confirmed my initial suspicions. Trevor Kipling, the senior officer investigating the murder of Mark Langley, had read the files on Alan Barnes, Neil Muir and Peter Stogneff, and felt the same way.

As one of the investigating detectives, I went and saw the parents the next evening. They told me about their son's disappearance. They had rung the police about an hour after he did not come home from the bus stop. They checked with Boris to make sure he had got home OK and learned that Richard had left him at the bus stop and that everything was normal when he left him. They checked with his girlfriend to make sure he had not gone there.

By now we were increasingly worried.

The following day was a Monday and the first door knocks late Monday morning produced nothing. People were at work and that meant we had to return to those addresses later to speak to these people. That was the first sign that the investigation was going to be difficult. Quick arrests happen when information from the scene is given to police almost straight away. A car number may be taken, someone knows a name or a face or someone rings the police with information. This didn't happen.

Our first decent bit of information came to us on Tuesday — two days after Richard had gone missing. The door knock had been widened. We had now covered alternative routes to the bus stop. The quickest way for Richard would have been straight down Ward Street and right into O'Connell Street. An alternative route was to turn right into Boulton Street about 50 metres from O'Connell Street and left into Marian Street to come out next to the delicatessen and bus stop.

Margaret Street was near the Kelvin's and certainly was not the shortest route to O'Connell Street but Trevor wanted to widen the search to make sure that we covered all possibilities. This move gave us our first bit of information. A young officer reported that a local resident living just around the corner from the Kelvin's had heard something unusual that Sunday evening.

'I was asleep in bed,' he said. 'I was suffering from the 'flu. I went to bed late that afternoon but some noises woke me about 6.15 p.m. I heard some cries for help and some car doors banging. There was a loud exhaust noise as the car accelerated away. I didn't think much of it at the time and went back to sleep.'

There was a university boarding college in Ward Street and a hotel in Margaret Street and unusual noises were heard all the time.

I couldn't believe it. The poor kid was fifty metres from his home and he had been grabbed and pushed in a car. He would have been rushing home for dinner when someone approached him.

Good on him, I thought. *At least he tried to resist.* But he was unlucky to have been snatched late on a Sunday afternoon in the streets of North Adelaide. Those streets are not exactly like Hindley Street nor those of Sydney's Kings Cross.

Now, at least this confirmed our thoughts that he had been abducted. He didn't just wander off. We were ninety-nine per cent sure but this news confirmed it.

By this time, Richard Kelvin's disappearance was declared a major crime, the same as the disappearances of all the boys. Declaration by police that a crime is considered major allows set procedures to occur and additional resources to be pulled from other sections of the police to assist with the investigation. A team leader is appointed and a primary investigatory team is nominated. The primary team is allocated the task of interviewing any suspects while secondary team members provide a supporting role. An exhibit officer is appointed to handle any property seized by detectives. The Major Crime Plan formalises each person's duties and allocates responsibilities. Trevor Kipling and I were nominated as the primary investigation team for the Kelvin disappearance. Trevor's previous partner, Paul Madden, had started working with Lin Strange as primary team members, investigating the unusual disappearance of Louise Bell, a young girl, from her bedroom in the southern suburbs. While this seemed a completely unconnected case at the time, it did sap police resources.

Trevor organised the crime scene examiners to attend Rob and Betteanne Kelvin's home after he went missing. They examined his bedroom and took samples of his hair from a brush. These hairs were obtained for comparison purposes if Richard's hairs were found at some other location, such as in a house or a car of a suspect. Also, we took one of Richard's schoolbooks, which had his handwriting in it, in case we received a ransom note.

As we normally do, police media requested assistance from the public and we received different bits of information. The most interesting phone call was from an anonymous caller saying that Richard Kelvin was being kept in a caravan in the hills. The call was a local one and when Adelaide people talk about the hills they are referring to the

Adelaide Hills, which extend roughly north and south for sixty-three kilometres just to the east of the city.

Where do you start when you are looking for a caravan in the Adelaide Hills? Was it a false lead? Were the abductors giving a false lead to divert police efforts in the wrong direction? Trevor assessed it as worthwhile. Besides, Alan Barnes had been dumped in the northern part of the Adelaide Hills at the South Para Reservoir. Mark Langley also had been dumped in the central Adelaide Hills. We weren't having much luck with any of the other leads, so we decided to concentrate on the hills north of Mount Lofty and also publicise that we were looking for a caravan. Obviously, that would alert Richard's abductors and they would have an opportunity to move him or even kill him. Making the decision to release the information was an extremely difficult one, but the area was so vast that police could not search it alone. Publicity was the best option, with the hope that something would happen. Trevor spoke to our boss, Chief Superintendent Gerry Edwards and the information went out.

Trevor and I spent some time in the emergency services helicopter, *Rescue One*, flying over the hills — over the Mt Crawford Forest and the towns of Kersbrook and Williamstown. A few caravans were spotted, but not that many. Besides, many would have been stored in sheds on different properties. The search was long and unrewarding.

Other detectives were added to the team to provide extra resources for the investigation. Among them were David Hunt, the son of the Commissioner of Police, and Peter Woite, the former footballer, who had played for Port Adelaide and

Glenelg. Peter won the Megary Medal for the best and fairest player in the South Australian football league.

On Sunday 24 July 1983, seven weeks after Richard Kelvin disappeared, the investigation took a real turn. Trevor Holmes was collecting moss rocks from the scrub adjacent to Mt Crawford Forest. The forest is situated in the northern Adelaide Hills, about two kilometres from the township of Kersbrook and about five kilometres from the reservoir where Alan Barnes was found. He was walking in the scrub next to a dirt and gravel airstrip that slopes down a ridge for 300 metres from the forest towards the coast. Crop-dusters used the airstrip to service the local rural community and the dirt road that ran diagonally from the airstrip towards the city was appropriately called Airstrip Road. Standing on the eastern edge of the airstrip, you could see the coast and tall chimneys of the Torrens Island power station that stood next to the Port River on the opposite side to Mutton Cove, where Neil Muir was found.

Richard was found about fifteen metres from the airstrip and about fifty metres from Airstrip Road. At the time anyone could drive from Airstrip Road straight onto the airstrip past the small sheep yard on the left. Now, a fence stops cars driving on the airstrip, and a locked gate allows access by forest rangers to the airstrip and the fire-track that runs off to the north alongside the edge of the forest.

Richard was lying on the ground on his left-hand side facing a blackboy bush. He was curled in the foetal position with his legs tucked up, almost nursing fronds of the bush. His head was bent forward, accentuating the arch of his curved back, with his arms to the front. His hands were almost on his stomach. He was wearing the same jeans and T-shirt that he sported when he disappeared. The Channel Nine logo stood out on the rear of his T-shirt, and the dog collar had been returned and was sitting firmly around his neck. If he didn't die there, it looked like one person had carried him to the blackboy bush with one arm under his legs and one arm under his arms before they placed him on the ground. If two people carried him into the bush, it would have been more likely that they would carry him by the arms and legs. If that was the case, when he was put down on the ground the body more likely would have been extended rather than in the foetal position.

I was familiar with the area. When I was riding police motorcycles, it was a boom time in motorcycle sport and a group of us formed a police motorcycle club. We rode the trails of Mt Crawford Forest. Within the forest, there were fire-trails that were large enough to take a motor vehicle and smaller tracks only large enough for walking or riding motorbikes.

If the killers had gone into the forest and dumped Richard, he probably would never have been found. Obviously, the abductors were not that concerned whether or not Richard was found. After the Alan Barnes and Neil Muir murders, they changed their *modus operandae* (the way criminals do things). With Alan Barnes and Neil Muir, the killers had a vehicle to take their bodies to water and dump them, hoping that they would disappear. The *modus operandae* for Peter Stogneff and Mark Langley was to use a vehicle and then dump them alongside a bush road. Richard Kelvin's dumping was similar to Peter Stogneff's and Mark Langley's. If the same people were involved, they had changed because dumping into water hadn't worked.

'I'll go with the body to the post-mortem.' Trevor said, more as a quiet order rather than a request. 'Can you tell the Kelvins that Richard has been found?'

Thanks very much, I thought. But I wasn't going to argue. Trevor was the boss — but what a job, telling Rob and Betteanne that their son's body had been found.

As with the other boys, Richard was taken in that same white van to the Forensic Science Centre where Dr Ross James performed the autopsy.

Trevor followed the van. Police are concerned with what we call the 'chain of evidence'. For example, when a body is found one of the detectives stays with the body to make sure that evidence is not contaminated. It is one way of stopping defence solicitors saying that something happened to the evidence from the time it was found till the forensic scientists took over.

No-one from the police likes attending post-mortems and some police say that there is no need for the investigating police to watch the body be cut open. They argue that the pathologist's report provides the information required by the police. But pathologists look at things differently from the police. Their emphasis is on the body and what might be wrong with it. The police perspective revolves more around the cause of any injuries and how they may have happened. Did a glass or wooden object cause the split anus? Were the saw marks made by a right- or left-handed person? This aspect is changing as pathologists have more and more knowledge about investigations but individual approaches are still different.

Dr James found that Richard had been undressed and redressed, and that he had the same injury to his anus as Alan Barnes, Neil Muir and Mark Langley. The forensic scientist could not say about anal injuries to Peter Stogneff because only his skeleton was found.

One job police hate more than attending a post-mortem examination is telling loved ones that a member of their family is dead. If the message is about a child, then it is even more difficult. Trevor got the better of the two jobs but it was a more efficient use of our time to do it that way; time is always important during a murder investigation.

I rang the buzzer on the wall outside Rob and Betteanne's home.

I didn't have a plan for how I was going to tell Rob and Betteanne. I had done it before, as all police officers have done in their careers, but telling a parent or a child that a family member has died is never easy.

On reflection, Rob and Betteanne must have realised that it would be a miracle if their son were still alive. There had been no ransom note. The chance that he had been kidnapped and was still alive was unlikely. As parents, they believed he had not run away, although parents can never be completely sure about these things.

All the indications were bad. Richard was happy with his new girlfriend and she had not heard from him. As well, there had been a run of terrible murders of young men. It all pointed to demons lurking in the city. Any news now would be bad.

Rob and Betteanne took me into the dining area and we sat down at their table. They didn't say anything and they let me lead the conversation.

I told both of them that we thought we had found their son. A boy had been found alongside an old airstrip near Kersbrook.

'We think that it is Richard,' I said and paused before continuing. 'The clothing is the same but we won't be 100 per cent sure until the identification is done.'

I still remember the conversation to this day. *Why didn't I say 'the boy' instead of 'it'?* I thought at the time. I wasn't being as sensitive as I could have been.

Rob and Betteanne sat still. They did not comment. There wasn't any outpouring of emotion. All of their tears had been shed in the weeks beforehand. They had just endured seven weeks of not knowing but suspecting the worse. Knowing would have been an unwelcome relief. Resignation showed in their faces and bodies. I was expecting to console Rob and Betteanne but what happened then surprised me. Tears welled up in my own eyes. I shouldn't have been surprised, I suppose, as my wife had been saying for some time that I was a softie. Here was this supposedly tough detective getting all emotional at the critical moment.

The conversation continued for another ten minutes as I explained what would happen from that point forward. The body needed to be formally identified as their son, a post-mortem would be performed and then Richard could be released to the family for burial. I asked about getting additional support for Rob and Betteanne and whether I could do anything for them. Of course, I couldn't. They had just been told that their son had been found dead next to a dirt airstrip in a lonely part of bush out of town. Their grieving had begun and the police officer investigating the murder was not the right person to be involved with that process. Someone else had to do that. I left and went back to the office trying to put that part of police work behind me.

Chapter 3

The Evidence

The police radios were quiet at 7.30 in the morning and the two officers who were allocated to guard the airstrip area overnight quickly passed over their log sheet to the next shift. The night had been uneventful and the two were tired and wanted to get home to bed. Guarding a murder scene in the middle of the night is not much fun, especially in a desolate area where no lights exist to brighten the area and remove the darkness. Newer officers are allocated the duty because they are still excited about being involved in a murder investigation even in a relatively small way and they can learn from the experience. The police guard is required to log the arrival of different people and anything of interest that happens in the general area. New men are more likely to remain observant and record events that might be missed by an older officer. Two police officers were present during the night to keep each other company but only one officer was present during the day because other people were around.

The new officer guarding the scene was busier, as different cars arrived and parked close by. He was first to arrive that next morning, stopping his patrol vehicle on the airstrip before walking to the police command vehicle, which had been parked just outside of the orange plastic bunting laying on the ground from the previous day. The bunting extended from the scrub onto the dirt and gravel of the airstrip and stretched down the strip for about forty metres before disappearing into the low bushes and small eucalyptus trees. The area where Richard Kelvin was found was still surrounded by the orange bunting, as police crime scene tape had not yet been introduced to South Australian police.

The police command vehicle was a converted Toyota van with a pop-top roof to allow greater movement inside the rear. Tables were installed and police radios fitted to the cupboards inside the van, which were accessed by sitting on the chairs on coasters, allowing the van to become a mini office. Command vehicles also carry generators to provide extra power for longer operations.

Trevor Kipling and I arrived early, parked our plain Mitsubishi sedan and waited for the others to arrive. As different police turned up they parked close to the bunting so they did not have carry their equipment too far, but not close enough to disturb any evidence the killers might have left. Crime scene examiners and the police photographers returned. Detectives came and left after having a look. Police media liaison was present to speak to the different news reporters who visited the site. At one stage fourteen vehicles lined up along the airstrip.

Trevor and I had assembled a busload of police cadets at the end of the airstrip just off the dirt road. There were thirty cadets in the police bus as well as the cadets' instructor, who parked alongside the other vehicles that had arrived earlier.

Trevor coordinated operations and asked me to work with the cadets and do a search down the dirt runway and in the scrub along the sides of the airstrip. I stepped onto the bus shortly after it arrived and spoke to the cadets, mainly fresh-faced young men, but there were a couple of women who wanted to have a go at policing. They were excited to be involved and to have an opportunity to get away from their classroom. Nowadays, police are more likely to use State Emergency Service volunteers to search around crime scenes because cadet training is so intensive over a six-month period that they cannot be spared to search crime scenes.

'We are going to search for evidence at a murder scene,' I said before explaining about Richard Kelvin and how he was abducted near his home before being found murdered.

'Solving a murder investigation is teamwork. You are now part of the team,' I continued, looking earnestly into their faces to make sure that everyone was listening intently. I didn't want anyone goofing off and missing any evidence.

'We are going to carry out an "emu parade" looking for any evidence that might solve this crime.'

I continued for about ten minutes, explaining that an emu parade took its name from the actions of the big bird slowly moving along and bobbing down searching for food. On this occasion the cadets would walk side by side searching for anything unusual. I would walk behind the line stopping their movement when anything was found and recording what, when and where anything of interest was found. Stopping the line made sure that the cadets stayed in a row, which lessened the possibility of them missing anything.

In scrub, things that catch the eye are generally man made. Such things as bullet shells, discarded clothing, a blanket used to wrap a body or even a discarded cigarette may provide some evidence or information about a crime. Other items can also be very important — such things as blood on the ground, a rock that has been moved and used as a bludgeon, or a heavy branch used as a club, which may have blood or hair on it.

The murder weapon in this case was something like a bottle with a tapered neck — similar to a beer bottle. This was hardly distinctive and couldn't be isolated like a gun or a bullet. The finding of a bullet shell can tell ballistic experts that it was an automatic rifle and, depending on the ammunition, even the type of weapon may be named.

The search took half a day. We looked outside the area surrounded by the bunting while crime scene examiners searched inside the area. Bottles were found but nothing to suggest that they had been used on the boy. They had been in the area too long or were the wrong shape. Papers were found but nothing to suggest that they belonged to Richard or the people who dumped him alongside the airstrip. A log was kept, recording the areas that were searched, the items discovered and what happened to those items.

Crime-scene examiners Ivan Sarvas, Tony Freckleton and Dave Russell minutely searched the ground where Richard Kelvin lay. They dug up the very small layer of grass and topsoil and sifted it through framed wire mesh to see if anything of interest was left behind. The crime-scene people look for jewellery, bullets, bullet cases — anything at all that belongs to the victim or the offender. Photographs recorded their precise work.

The only other thing that was of interest to the crime scene examiners was a dead, maggot-infested dog that had been dumped not far away from Richard. Tony Freckleton almost stepped on it. There was nothing to suggest that the dog had any link to Richard, but both bodies had fly larvae on them, and if it could be learned when the dog was dumped, then the life cycle of the maggots might give an idea of when Richard was dumped. If we could be certain when he was dumped, then we could appeal to people visiting the forest at that time to learn whether or not they had seen anything unusual, like a vehicle parked strangely, or people loitering in the area. Knowing when someone was killed or dumped allows police to narrow their investigation. It makes the investigation more manageable. Taking the stinking dog away for examination shows the lengths that police and crime scene examiners will go to when investigating a serious case. Can you imagine the smell in their clothes and car as they took the dog to the South Australian Museum for further examination?

There was no evidence around Richard Kelvin's body — the same as the other boys. There was no sign of a struggle or violence occurring at the airstrip. This indicated that they weren't murdered at the location where their bodies were found.

Trevor didn't say anything as we drove back to the office. He didn't have to. I knew what he was thinking.

Where were they killed? Probably a house somewhere but where?

I was driving and waiting for Trevor to come up with some ideas about where to go from here but he didn't say anything. I didn't have much to offer, either. It was a sombre drive back to Adelaide — he sat there as I slid on the corners of the dirt road that ran down Snake Gully towards Golden Grove as we returned to Adelaide.

Snake Gully. What a name.

I'd been this way before and thought the name gave a touch of interest to the area when I rode it as a part of *The Advertiser* 24-Hour Motor Cycle Trial in the 1970s. But now it presented a different picture and made me think of the killers within Adelaide's community.

These people are worse than snakes and more slippery. We are going to need a big break to solve these murders.

Most murder cases are solved because the victim knows the offender. If you are going to be murdered, then the chances are that you will be murdered by your partner, your mate or somebody who lives nearby. Police often solve these murders because they are crimes of passion, where an argument occurs, a lover is taken, or people turn violent on one another. Invariably the murderer is known, and often he or she confesses or another person is present and sees what has happened.

A murder committed by a stranger is much more difficult for the police to solve. Investigations like this are invariably a 'hard slog'. What did we have to investigate with the boys? Five butchered bodies, no murder scenes and no murder weapon left behind that might provide some evidence — that's what we had. A knife left behind may have fingerprints or some of the offender's blood on it. A gun might have been registered at police Firearms Branch. We had nothing. Also, it appeared that these were 'stranger murders', in which the victims did not know their killers.

The similarities between the murders were striking, indicating that with three of them, and possibly with all five, the same people were involved. These stranger murders appeared to be planned and callous. Muir, like the others, had an anal injury, but he had been cut similarly to Peter Stogneff. That aspect about his murder was different from those of Alan Barnes, Mark Langley and Richard Kelvin.

Were all the murders linked? Or were those of Alan Barnes, Mark Langley and Richard Kelvin linked but not those of Neil Muir and Peter Stogneff? Was more than one person involved? It appeared so but we could not be certain. All of these questions did not have clear answers and made the investigation more difficult.

The circumstances surrounding the murders were interesting. Firstly, three of the boys were last seen on a Sunday.

Alan Barnes was last seen on Sunday 17 June 1979 and found on Sunday 24 June 1979, one week later. The post-mortem revealed that he had not been killed straight away, but in the forty-eight hours before he was found. Also, shortly before he was killed, he had been hit with some type of blunt object; there was a circular abrasion around his right eye and intense bruising of his right eyelid. He was beaten as well as abused.

The examination showed that rigor mortis — where the body stiffens — had set in and was starting to wear off. Alan was probably killed on the Friday and dumped on the Saturday. He wasn't killed straight away. What was he doing for the week after he was seen hitchhiking? Was he kept captive or was he with someone voluntarily? If he was kept captive, where was he kept?

Mark Langley disappeared in the very early hours of a Sunday morning, on 28 February 1982, and he was found one week and one day later. He disappeared after Peter Stogneff but was found before him. Severe putrefaction had occurred before he was found. The soft tissue under the skin that was exposed to the sun had almost disappeared due to February's heat working on the body. Mark's head was almost reduced to just the skull and the soft tissues around his neck were totally destroyed. Jeans covered his lower body and putrefaction there had just started. Because of the state of his body the time of death was not certain but pathology suggested he died at least five days earlier. Was he killed immediately after he went missing? If not, where was he on the Sunday, Monday, Tuesday and possibly Wednesday?

Richard Kelvin also went missing on a Sunday. He was found seven weeks later, on a Sunday. As well as the anal injuries he had sustained, he had injuries to his head, back and one buttock. Pathologist Ross James' assessment of Richard's head injury was enlightening. He had received a blow to the head very early in his captivity, which had caused a subdural haemorrhage — bleeding between the brain and skull. The blow could have killed him but he recovered from his injury. Trevor and I felt that the blow could have been inflicted when he first was grabbed in North Adelaide — we knew that he resisted being dragged into the car. His cries for help showed that. The pathology findings indicated he was probably hit around the head when his abductors first grabbed him and forced him into the car.

When Ross James checked Richard's body, he found a deep-seated bruise on the left side of his back inflicted two or three weeks before his death. The bleeding into the tissues of the back had stopped and the colour of the bruise had changed, allowing Ross to estimate when Richard was hit. There was another deep-seated bruise to his right buttock caused several days before his death. The bastards had beaten Richard as well as abusing him during his captivity.

Neil Muir and Peter Stogneff did not fit with the theory about Sunday. Just over one month after Alan Barnes went missing, Neil Muir was killed. He was last seen on Monday 27 August 1979 and his body found on the next day, at Mutton Cove. He was probably killed on the Monday and dumped in the early hours of the Tuesday morning. Obviously, the people who grabbed Neil Muir could have had an extra day off work but his disappearance varied the pattern. Peter Stogneff's case was also different.

Peter Stogneff was the third to go. He followed Alan Barnes and Neil Muir. Not on a Sunday this time or the day immediately after a weekend. He wagged school on Thursday 28 August 1981. We could never be sure when he was dumped because Peter was found nearly a year after he went missing. There was insufficient information gathered from Peter's remains to determine when he was murdered. Was he held captive also?

The similarities between the killings were numerous. The people who murdered Barnes, Langley and Kelvin most likely worked during the week and had Sundays off to ply their terrible trade in mutilation.

Barnes, Muir, Langley and Kelvin all had similar injuries to their anuses that most likely caused their deaths. The bare bones of Peter Stogneff did not reveal any injuries to his skin, tissue and muscle but the saw marks left on his bones and the fact that he was a good looking young man suggested that he, too, probably had been abused before being killed.

All of the young men would have lost one hell of a lot of blood. Alan Barnes, Mark Langley and Richard Kelvin were wearing clothes that were not stained by blood. Also, their bodies showed no dried blood. Blood obviously had been wiped from their bodies. This meant that they had been undressed to some degree, abused and then redressed. The redressing was confirmed because Mark Langley's belt was replaced in the loops of his pants the wrong way around. The belt buckle was on the right-hand side of the zip instead of the left, where all men place their buckles. Also, his pants were done up but his zip was still undone.

Neil Muir was not redressed. He was not wearing any clothes. His corpse was bizarre enough without having any clothes put back on it. His new clothes consisted of the garbage bags he was dumped in. We could not tell with Peter Stogneff. He and Neil Muir were sawn apart and discarded.

All of the cleaning and cutting meant that the young mens' bodies had been washed at some stage or that their body parts had been washed anyway. Cleaning and washing a body generally means water, and a large amount of it would have been needed to clean up all the blood and mess caused.

Most people would not comprehend the amount of mess that comes from a body. Television has sanitised our senses because it can't show all the sights and smells present at some crime scenes. The media shows blood as a stain on a shirt or a small pool on the ground. The loss of most of a person's blood can never be shown on television. Television reporters and camera operators see but cannot show the splattering of blood and brains over the walls of a room when someone is shot in the head. A camera and small screen cannot convey the smell and sight of urine and faeces when body fluids are emptied as muscles relax and die.

The use of a home bathroom or laundry was possible in this case. The victims may have been put naked in a bath to clean them. A murderer is unlikely to put a body on his rear lawn and hose his victim down. But what if the murders happened at a business premises where water and a cleaning area were available — a slaughter house, a butcher's shop or a factory? We couldn't discount any of these possibilities.

The dumping of the boys most likely occurred at night, using a car. The South Para Bridge from where Alan Barnes was dropped, probably during the very early hours of Sunday morning, was on a relatively busy road between Kersbrook and Williamstown. The road is still busy on Friday nights with young people driving around. The very early hours of the morning allow approaching vehicles to be heard. At night sounds travel further and car lights are turned on. The stillness allows the senses to detect approaching people or vehicles that may interrupt evil plans. The darkness of night hides killers' activities and masks their vehicles.

There had to be a big strong man involved or more than one person. Lifting a body from the back seat or boot of a car and then over a railing higher than a metre was possible for one person but unlikely.

Alan Barnes had been missing one week and there were injuries to his anus and back. But his body was still fresh. Decomposition had not started.

Neil Muir was found the day after he disappeared. He had been cut up, but death was recent and decay of his remaining tissues had not started. Neil Muir's dumping also most likely occurred at night, and a car used. There was nothing to suggest he was killed at Mutton Cove. He was killed somewhere else. He was cast off in an isolated spot but still within the inner metropolitan area. Therefore he had to be taken to that spot. Neil Muir's bag was caught on the rocks indicating that the low tide in the Port River could not be seen when he was dropped. This also suggested that Neil Muir was dumped at night.

Peter Stogneff's case was more difficult to determine. Peter Stogneff was a mystery. A time of death could not be established. When he was dumped was a mystery. The physical evidence had disappeared with time and in the heat of the flames of the fire lit by the farmer. Like Neil Muir he was cut up, which made it possible for one person to dispose of the bodies because of their smaller size.

Similar arguments about the use of a vehicle and the night applied to Mark Langley. Mark was found on a Monday, just over a week after he disappeared. His body had started to putrify because of the heat of February, and most likely he was dumped early in the week shortly after he was killed — possibly the Sunday or Monday night.

Richard Kelvin's case was even more difficult to fathom. He was found seven weeks after he went missing and the arguments about night time and the use of a vehicle still applied. He was abducted on a Sunday, and found on a Sunday. The work of the pathologist and a woman we called the 'Maggot Lady' told us when he was dumped at the airstrip.

The Maggot Lady was Beryl Morris, an entomologist from the South Australian museum. She made comparisons between the maggots on the dog and on Richard. Beryl, an attractive woman, studied flies, hence her unfortunate nickname, but it clearly explained what she did, which I had never heard of until I met her. She was a wonderful professional who was easy to get on with. She played a small but important role in the investigation, as many others did. Beryl used the life cycle of flies to help determine when Richard Kelvin was dumped. Maggots were on Richard's body and determining their age could indicate when the flies first started laying their eggs. Richard would have been dumped about that time but additional information was needed to assist with this task. We needed information about the dead dog and the local weather conditions.

A door knock of the local farms did not discover any information about people hanging around the area, but when police spoke to the locals, questions were also asked about the dead dog. Did anyone know anything about it? Whose dog was it? When was it dumped? We didn't find out who dumped the dog but we had a minor success when Tony Freckleton, the keen, sharp crime examiner, who attended the airstrip, learned from one of the farmers that the dog had been thrown out three weeks before Richard was found.

Records from the Woods and Forests Department helped with weather information but the records of a local woman provided extra detail the Maggot Lady needed. Ivan Sarvas had come across a farmer near the airstrip who collected details of weather conditions, which included the amount of rainfall on her farm. These extra pieces of information assisted Beryl with her task but such inquiries take time and effort, and show how much effort was put into the investigation to provide the greatest possible amount of information, and the vital clues to solve the murders.

The decomposition of Richard's body and the work of Beryl Morris indicated that he was dumped about two weeks beforehand and killed shortly before he was dumped — possibly on Sunday, 10 July 1983. If he was dumped then and snatched on Sunday, 5 June, where was Richard Kelvin for five weeks? Five weeks! It was an unbelievable length of time to be held captive. Where was he kept? The physical handling of the boys' bodies indicated that more than one person was involved, and now, with Richard, that possibility was more likely. The length of time that he was kept alive indicated that more than one person had to be around to assist with feeding and keeping him under control. But we couldn't be certain — other individuals have kept people caged over long periods of time.

The location of the bodies gave more clues about the killers. The first two bodies were dumped into water or, more accurately, the killers tried to dispose of the bodies into water. Alan Barnes was flung from the bridge into the dry South Para Reservoir, and Neil Muir was dropped into the low tide of the Port River about seventeen kilometres to the north-west of the city but within the metropolitan area. After the first two bodies were found, not hidden by water, if the same people were involved, did the killers not worry about trying to dispose of evidence of their crime in water? The other boys, who were murdered after Alan Barnes and Neil Muir, were simply left by the side of the road.

Other similarities were simple: Alan Barnes, Mark Langley and Richard Kelvin all were dumped in the Adelaide Hills. Mark Langley was closer to the city, about twelve kilometres away slightly to the south-east, but in the Adelaide Hills. Alan Barnes and Richard Kelvin were also left in the Adelaide Hills, Richard's body being found in the same general area as Alan Barnes. The dumping sites indicated that the murderers lived in the greater Adelaide area, possibly on the northern side.

Trevor Kipling collated the information as we went along. The following table outlines the events as we knew them.

	Barnes	Muir	Stogneff	Langley	Kelvin
Last seen	Sunday	Monday	Thursday	Sunday	Sunday
When found	Sunday	Tuesday	Wednesday	Monday	Sunday
Date last seen	17 June 1979	27 August 1979	27 August 1981	28 February 1982	5 June 1983
Date found	24 June 1979	28 August 1979	23 June 1982	8 March 1982	24 July 1983
Injury	Anal	Anal	N/K	Anal	Anal
Other injury	Eye injury, broken bones	Head injury, dissected	Dissected	Incision	Head injury, brusing
Redressed	Yes	No	N/K	Yes	Yes
Vehicle used	Yes	Yes	Yes	Yes	Yes
Location where dumped	North-east	North-west	North	East	North-east
Property missing	No	Yes	Yes	Yes	No

Trevor was trying to fathom this information when another detective in the Major Crime Squad, Lee Haddon, received information about the murder of Neil Muir.

Chapter 4

The Arrest of Dr Millhouse

Neil Muir was a druggie but he didn't deserve to die. He was the oldest of the butchered boys and at twenty-five, a man rather than a boy. He moved around, and lived with a mate at Unley 'til shortly after his mate went to jail for possessing housebreaking implements. He lived with a girlfriend at Kilburn for a while but just before he was killed he was sleeping on the floor of a dosshouse in Carrington Street in the centre of Adelaide.

During 1979 he was on a downward spiral from his drug use. His friends said he was looking the worse for wear. He had been abusing narcotics for six years, having started when he was nineteen. He first sought help at a methadone clinic in 1978, but Neil Muir was like so many druggies — the methadone just became another drug to use and abuse.

The clinic assessed Neil Muir as having a moderate physical dependence on opiates. He was being treated with methadone but when he complained about general discomfort and agitation from withdrawal, he was given Clonidine, an antihypertensive drug, and Rohypnol, a sedative and an hypnotic.

On the Friday, three days before he disappeared, he was at the methadone clinic at Hillcrest Hospital in a northern suburb of Adelaide. He was wearing a distinctive bulky knit cardigan, bone coloured, with black stripes running through it. The cardigan complemented his light-coloured cord jeans. An ebony bangle was on his wrist, and a sleeper was in one earlobe and a drop-earing in his other ear. He carried a flick knife. None of these items have been found.

Neil Muir, like Alan Barnes, was good looking but he had softer features than Alan Barnes. Neil Muir's long brown hair and light beard tended to elongate his face, which was thinning from poor nutrition resulting from his drug habit. He was a poly (multiple) drug user. He abused heroin, methadone and barbiturates.

While Neil Muir's murder was similar, with an anal injury, there were no other linkages to suggest it was connected to Alan Barnes'. Neil Muir was cut up while Alan Barnes was intact. They did not know each other so the common thread of being killed by an associate was discounted. Initially, Neil Muir's killing was thought to be drug related. Neil Muir owed some money around town for drugs that he had scored. One theory related to the possibility that he was killed because he had not paid his debts. Detective Rod Hunter and others who were investigating the Alan Barnes' murder were working on the possibility that he was murdered by the family of a girl that he allegedly raped. His anal injuries were thought to be a sadistic sexual payback. Over time we learnt this was not the case.

Major Crime and police generally were still basking in the success of Glen Lawrie and Peter Foster solving the Truro serial killings and, at that time, there was nothing to suggest we had another run of killings starting. John Woite and Lee Haddon were the detective sergeants working on Glen Lawrie's team in the Major Crime Squad. John was tall — a big man in height and size. He was very methodical with his investigations. Lee was an older detective, single and dedicated to his work like most of the detectives at Major Crime. Lee Haddon was working on the murder of Neil Muir. The things that differentiated the detectives in the squad were their intelligence, experience and how much the pressure had got to them from their years as detectives. The pressure did not come so much from the amount of physical work although, often, long hours were worked; it was from the stress from having to perform and get results case after case.

There is always pressure on the Major Crime Squad when a murder occurs, especially when an old, very young, or some prominent person is murdered. There were the usual killings — a man was killed after a family argument at Waterloo Corner and a man was knifed and killed at

Modbury. However, the murder of Derrence Stevenson, a homosexual lawyer, was the most unusual case.

Derrence Stevenson was murdered by his young boyfriend and stuffed in his food freezer. The Stevenson house and office on Greenhill Road was notable for its unusual design. The house was built on a triangular block on Greenhill Road, near Glen Osmond Road. It filled most of the block and not only was the house triangular but the roof rose to form a three-sided pyramid. The case is memorable because of the design of the house and the use of the freezer to hide the body.

The young boyfriend put the lawyer in the freezer and then used superglue to stick the lid down before he took his car and headed to Coober Pedy, the opal town in the far north of the State. The freezing of the body did not allow a time of death to be accurately obtained from body temperature. When a body is found relatively soon after death the pathologist places a thermometer into the anus to find the body temperature. After death, rigor mortis sets in and, also, the body cools at a steady rate. After so many hours the body temperature will be at so many degrees. By freezing the body the cooling process is interrupted and so time of death cannot be determined.

Here was another man murdered in a bizarre way. These killings seemed to be the start of something very strange in the quiet, conservative State of South Australia.

Not everyone thought Neil Muir was killed by druggies who wanted their money. The dissection of his body would just have been going too far. Lee Haddon wanted to keep his options open, so he sought help via a new science which was just starting in the 1970s.

Criminal profiling had been receiving a great deal of publicity at the time. Profiling was refined and marketed by the FBI in America but other law enforcement agencies in the 1970s were experimenting with it as well. The South Australia Police Department also tried it when Neil Muir was found. The crime was so different and so bizarre it warranted a try. So, detectives from Major Crime asked the police department's psychologists to have a go at it after Neil Muir was found.

Most large police departments have psychologists working for them. However, they are not employed to do criminal profiling, as people may first think. Their primary role is to help police to recruit suitable people and also to help those recruits later in their careers. They help police deal with the stress from their work that can occur at different times. These problems may be from work or from stress caused by working in an hierarchical organisation, stress from marriage breakdowns or from drinking too much.

Lee Haddon received two reports from the police psychologists. Ray Dowd, university educated and the son of a police officer, furnished his report on 31 August 1979. Ray believed that Neil Muir's murder was not a crime of passion in which the murderer lost control. If that was the case, Ray felt that extreme anger, hatred or fear would have affected the killer. Such emotions usually result in injuries to the head or body, with a number of wounds inflicted in a very short time. Neil Muir had received a blow to the head but there was no evidence of multiple blows to the head or body or multiple knife-wounds.

Ray felt that the killer might be psychotic — the murderer might have had a severe mental derangement involving the whole personality. Psychotic behaviour could be drug induced and Ray recommended investigating Neil Muir's association with other drug users. Because Alan Barnes may have died in a similar way, he recommended that common associates be considered. As with Alan Barnes, it soon became obvious that this was not the case and speculation of Alan Barnes and Neil Muir being killed by the same person or group was starting.

Ray theorised that the killer might be a homosexual who had strong sexual fantasies. He considered the deliberate and meticulous mutilation of the body, which could have taken up to three hours, as completing some kind of plan. He also considered the insertion of an object similar to a tapered bottle into the anus. The pathologist, Ross James, was talking about the possibility that if it was a beer bottle, the metal cap had still been on it, causing some of the tearing. Ray considered this and the cutting up of the penis and the removal of the testicles to be part of the acting out of aggressive sexual fantasies. He thought that cutting off the fingers may have occurred because they were considered phallic objects. The mutilation was compared with the Boston Strangler, who also mutilated his victims.

There was a lack of agreement between the professionals as to whether or not the mutilation was done with some professional knowledge and skill. Ray Dowd worked on the advice that there was some skill involved. He said that the semi-professional nature of some of the cuts suggested that the killer could be a person with a medical or para-medical background or in a job where knowledge of the joints and cuts could be learned. The difficulty was that on 30 August 1979, the Chief Meat Inspector for the abattoirs gave a statement. He had expert knowledge about boning and skinning of animals. He believed that the skinning was not consistent with a person having any expertise in this area. It was done in a rough manner. He also observed roughness in the area of the legs where the muscular tissue was removed. Boning skills were not present. He said that a saw was used on the bone while a knife was used on the flesh. This meant that the person who butchered Neil Muir was not likely to be an employee of an abattoir. This did help Lee narrow things a bit but not that much.

Ray Dowd also kept his options open with his assessment. He suggested an alternative hypothesis: that much of the mutilation was done to reduce the possibility of identifying the victim. If the victim could be identified, then a suspect who was close to the victim could be identified. He argued the possibility that the cutting up was to disguise the identity of the body but the offenders' resolve weakened as their gruesome task continued. Ray suggested that, in the end, they just wanted to get rid of it.

Ray was keeping his options open, which was fair enough, as criminal profiling was in its infancy. However, I had doubts about Ray's alternative hypothesis. The tying of the body together with clothesline, stuffing it into plastic bags and taking it to Mutton Cove still indicated resolve and organisation enough to complete the disposal. Also, Neil

Muir's head had not been butchered in any way. His facial features were clearly intact. It was very likely he could be identified from his head alone but that wasn't needed. Neil Muir's fingers were left with his body and they were used to obtain fingerprints, which identified Neil. The killer could have easily disposed of them separately.

Ray Dowd also considered the possibility of a payback killing for Neil's drug debts around town. This could not be ignored; nor could the idea that Alan Barnes' murder was a payback killing. All of these theories expanded the possibilities that Major Crime had to cover. The motive for Neil Muir's killing was not clear, and lack of a clear motive did not help lessen the number of areas to check for suspects.

Prosecutors like to prove a motive in murder cases. This helps 'sell' the case to jurors. If the jury can see that a murder happened because of a jealous rage, to cover up a rape or a robbery to get money for drugs then the case is much stronger. The law doesn't require the police or prosecutors to prove a motive but it is better if they do. Motive helps convince the jury that the accused committed the crime.

Milton Kelly, the head of the Psychology Unit, followed with another report on 4 September 1979. Milton was not a police officer but he had many years' experience in the police organisation. He considered Ray Dowd's report and clarified several points. Milton stressed that the offender may not be mentally ill — may not be pyschotic. Milton Kelly did not discount the possibility of the killer being mentally ill but he extended the possibilities. He felt that if the person was not mentally ill, he would very likely be an extremely sadistic psychopath — a person with abnormal social behaviour.

He felt this because of the deliberate and controlled way the killer mutilated and disposed of Neil Muir. He theorised that the acting out of sexual or violent fantasies might have absorbed the person to such an extent that the butcherer may not have related to the corpse as another human being. He considered that the killer might not openly display a violent or aggressive personality and considered that the murderer might be seen as polite, gentle and passive to other people. The person would be seen as conventional and his personal habits characterised by neatness and cleanliness.

Milton listed the characteristics of a psychopathic person as:

- Non-conformist
- Egocentric and selfish with a lack of loyalties
- Having no conscience and no anxiety or remorse for his actions
- Manipulative
- Incapable of love and affection
- Impulsive
- Incapable of learning from past experiences
- Callous and sadistic
- Possibly charming and likeable
- An accomplished liar

A psychopath can receive a lot of sadistic or sexual pleasure, or a combination of both, from torturing and mutilating his victims. Milton said that the offender might not know a victim and the person might be selected at random. However, Milton also had a bet each way. He gave an alternative view that the victim may have been well known to the killer and that Neil Muir was dissected to punish him for real or imagined insults.

All of this information did not help Lee Haddon get any closer to his killer. The killer could be mentally ill, but he also could be a psychopath. Also, there was the possibility of drug debts, which Lee was already aware of and, finally, the offender may have been an associate or a stranger. This comment was not to denigrate the police psychologists but we had to keep our options open. As I said, criminal profiling was very new.

The pressure on detectives to solve the Neil Muir murder was always present but hadn't risen to the extent to which people were being stressed. Lee Haddon was working on the Muir matter and things began to look promising when one person came to the attention of the police. Two telephone calls were received about a person who could have killed Neil Muir. This time the calls were not anonymous. Two druggies were prepared to give statements, and their names and who they thought might have done it.

That person, they alleged, was Peter Leslie Millhouse, a doctor from Mount Gambier in the south-east of the state. He was forty-five and single. He claimed to be a distant relative of Robin Millhouse, flamboyant Attorney-General with the Liberal government, Army Reserve officer and, after he left politics, a judge. The doctor was a general practitioner with degrees in medicine and surgery, although he did not do much surgery.

Millhouse lived in rented accommodation and drove a ten-year-old Holden. His leased Mercedes had gone and he wasn't exactly making a lot of money as a doctor. When Neil Muir was killed, Dr Millhouse was living in a single-fronted attached house in Stanley Street, North Adelaide. The cottage was one of a dozen attached cottages, all refurbished in the same style. The blue stone sparkled under the veranda, which stepped out onto the small front yard, which was separated from the street by the low front fence. The fence was made of metal latticework, which is unusual for Adelaide. The white latticework matched the white wooden doors and white wooden window frames bordered by white shutters.

The front door on the left of the cottage opened to the passageway and rooms spread from the right-hand side of the passageway. The passageway ran the full length of the house to the courtyard garden out the back. The backyard was run down and uninteresting. A clothesline ran down the side of the rear yard, the lawn was overgrown but a large plane tree filled the opposite side and provided the dull yard with some colour.

Peter Millhouse was an alcoholic and his life was complicated even further by his homosexuality. He had realised that he was a homosexual in puberty and, as his preferences developed, he found he was having sex with men who were not well known to him. He would hang around hotels in Hindley Street and although he looked for company, he was a loner with few friends.

Doctor Millhouse had known Neil Muir for about four years but Lee found no evidence, statements or photographs to prove they had actually had sex. Neil Muir chased Millhouse for drugs but no evidence could be found to show that Millhouse supplied them to him. However, at the time Neil Muir was killed, Doctor Millhouse was worried that he might be in trouble for supplying prescriptions to other druggies.

Neil Muir initially was thought to have disappeared on that Sunday in August 1979. Doctor Millhouse and Neil Muir were together on Neil's last Sunday. He was drinking with Peter Millhouse at the Hope Inn Sports and Social Club in the inner western suburb of Ridleyton. The old club was like Neil Muir and Peter Millhouse — all of them were showing signs of neglect. The long rectangular building was clean and neat but had seen better days. Its front fence of galvanized pipe and wire mesh was bent and broken.

After more investigation, Lee Haddon learned that a bouncer in one of Neil Muir's regular haunts had seen him on the Monday. The bouncer at the Mediterranean Hotel knew Muir as a regular. He had seen him with Dr Millhouse on the evenings of Thursday and Friday, 23 and 24 August 1979. They were at their usual table in the front bar, next to the jukebox, drinking schooners of beer. On the Monday — the day before he died, Neil Muir was by himself back at the Mediterranean Hotel.

Neil Muir arrived at about 1.30 in the afternoon wearing a long sleeved shirt with his brown corduroy jeans. His hair, goatie beard and moustache were worn exactly as shown in the photograph that Lee Haddon was using to show to people. Neil sat at his usual table and drank schooners until the waitress said to the bouncer:

'One drunk sleeping at the table.'

The bouncer went to Neil Muir, picked him up and took him to the street.

'I'm going mate. I'm going,' said the quiet druggie and he swayed down the street heading for Morphett Street.

Neil Muir was next seen dressed in a garbage bag laying on the rocks of Mutton Cove.

In the days following Neil Muir's murder, Dr Peter Millhouse was on a bender. However, this did not stop him contacting well-known criminal lawyer, Peter Waye, about his problems. He sought legal advice on that Friday and on the next day, on the advice of his colleagues, Dr Millhouse booked himself into Osmond House, a rehabilitation clinic in the eastern suburbs.

On 3 September 1979, Lee Haddon spoke with Dr Millhouse at Osmond House. The doctor produced his letter from Peter Waye saying that he didn't want to answer any questions. Obviously, this made Lee Haddon even more suspicious.

Crime scene police examined the untidy house of the doctor. Witnesses were found who said that large garbage bags, similar to those used to clothe the body of Neil Muir, had been in the house. The yellow cord that tied him together was the same type that is used on clotheslines that are extended out and attached to a pole. That type of cord was no longer on the clothesline. A type of twine had replaced it. But the bags and the clotheslines were very common and were in the homes and backyards of many thousands of people. Also, Lee could not prove when the line was changed. It may have happened well before

Dr Millhouse moved into the house. Witnesses were not clear in their evidence about the clothesline. All of this did not help Lee with his circumstantial case.

When Lee searched the doctor's home, initial testing of the bathroom indicated blood had been on the floor but it could not be grouped because of the use of cleaners on it. Grouping of the blood would have told whether or not it was the blood of Neil Muir. Doctor Millhouse had a cleaner at the time and that she cleaned the bathroom at about the time of the murder and she said that she wiped away marks on the wall similar to blood spots.

A Bandaid was found with the remains of Neil Muir. Its sticky paste held some fibres and they were sent to forensics for examination and Anna Parabyk, analyst from the Forensic Science Centre, compared the fibres with those from a rug in Millhouse's cottage. Although she could not say that they were from the rug, they were similar in every respect.

On 20 November 1979, Dr Millhouse was working in the country town of Whyalla. By this time, Lee was convinced that the doctor was his man and he drove to the town with two other detectives, Wayne Warnest and Dave Mullins. They arrested Dr Millhouse at the Eyre Hotel where he was staying, with a warrant that had been issued over the misuse of prescriptions. The four of them travelled overnight back to Adelaide together. By this time, Millhouse had one of Peter Waye's standard letters saying that his client did not wish to speak to police. Lee's hands were tied. He wanted to speak to Millhouse while they were travelling back to Adelaide.

❂ ❂ ❂

Lee was working on the theory that someone close to Neil Muir had killed him. On Thursday, 17 January 1980, with the evidence he had, Lee Haddon went to Mount Gambier with Detective Bob Lindner and drove to the home of Dr Millhouse's parents, where he was staying at the time. Lee Haddon recorded his conversation with the doctor.

'Dr Millhouse — Sergeant Haddon, Detective Lindner, Major Crime Squad.'

'Yes, I remember you.'

'I'm still making enquiries into the death of Neil Muir. I still want to ask you questions in relation to this death. Are you now prepared to answer questions that I put to you?'

'Look gentlemen, I must still take the advice of my solicitor and not answer any questions.'

'Last time I spoke to you on the way to Adelaide from Whyalla, you told me that you wanted to answer my questions and that you'd go to your solicitor and request that you be allowed to answer questions. Did you not?'

'Yes, I said that.'

'Did you approach your solicitor about making a statement?'

'I tried to get him a couple of times on the phone but he was out.'

'Are you prepared at this stage to answer any questions relating to the death of Muir?'

'I'm sorry. I must take the advice of my solicitor and decline to answer any questions. It's my fundamental right.'

'I'm now arresting you on a charge of murder relating to the death of Neil Frederick Muir. You don't have to say anything in answer to this charge unless you want to but anything you do say may be given in evidence. Do you understand the charge?'

'This is ridiculous. I told you I didn't know the man. I don't know anything about it.'

Dr Millhouse became upset and called out to his mother and father. Lee let Dr Millhouse speak to Peter Waye on the phone before taking him to the Mount Gambier Police Station where he was charged, photographed, fingerprinted and put in one of the cells. He was charged with having murdered Neil Federick Muir on or about 27 August 1979 at North Adelaide or elsewhere.

The charge indicated the weakness of Lee's case. He could not be sure exactly where Neil Muir was killed even though there were indications of blood in the bathroom. Also, he could not say exactly when he had been killed.

Lee could prove that they knew each other, and blood had been found in the bathroom of Peter Millhouse's rented premises in North Adelaide. At the doctor's trial, the prosecutor argued that the dissection of Muir had to have been done by someone who had some medical training and knowledge of anatomy. Dr Robert Britten-Jones gave this evidence but he couldn't say if the person who did the dissection was a doctor.

Dr Millhouse was still saying that he didn't know Neil Muir. Lee could prove that he did know Neil Muir.

Dr Millhouse's arrest removed the spotlight from the investigation into Alan Barnes' murder. Police speculated that the same offender or offenders committed both murders. Both victims were abusing drugs. Both suffered anal injuries but these similarities were not enough to link both murders to one offender or group of offenders.

Dr Millhouse endured two trials. The first trial started on 29 July 1980 but, less than a month later, the judge, Justice Williams, suffered a heart attack. The jury was dismissed and a new trial started on 2 September 1980, with a new judge and jury. The second trial commenced with Justice Mohr controlling proceedings. The trial lasted twenty-four days, and ninety-eight witnesses gave evidence.

Towards the end of the trial, Dr Millhouse took the unusual step of giving evidence under oath. Most often in murder cases defendants refuse to give evidence; in those days they could give an unsworn statement from the dock and the prosecutor was not allowed to cross-examine the defendant. But Peter Millhouse allowed himself to be cross-examined. He gave sworn evidence over three days, a long time to be giving evidence. He was cross-examined for a full day by the bespectacled prosecutor, Tony Bishop.

Tony Bishop, a car enthusiast from the Office of the Director of Public Prosecutions, conducted the case against Millhouse. After Dr Millhouse gave sworn evidence, Tony addressed the jury. He said that the prosecution's case was based on circumstantial evidence because there wasn't any direct evidence implicating the accused with the crime. Circumstantial evidence inferred he was involved rather than anyone saying that they saw him do it. Tony Bishop summed up by saying that the prosecution case rested on eleven points.

1. The type of relationship between the two men indicated Millhouse could have committed the crime;

2. Alleged false denials by Millhouse;
3. The association between the victim and the accused was on-going at the time of the murder;
4. The person who mutilated Neil Muir had anatomical and medical knowledge;
5. Evidence indicating that Neil Muir had been at Dr Millhouse's home;
6. Yellow cord binding the body was similar to the line that had been on Dr Millhouse's clothesline;
7. Plastic bags similar to those that Neil Muir was stuffed into were in the cottage;
8. Use of Doctor Millhouse's car and denials about its use;
9. General behaviour and conduct of Millhouse;
10. Opportunity to commit the murder; and
11. Motive to commit the murder.

Tony Bishop provided two possible motives for the mutilation of Neil Muir. Firstly, he adopted one of the views of the police psychologist and said that the mutilation could have been done out of contempt. Secondly, it was done to help dispose of the body. However, a problem occurred with the blood found in the bathroom. Scientific tests showed it was blood but even though it could not be matched completely, its grouping showed it was more likely to have came from a druggie shooting up in the doctor's house — this was a major weakness in Lee's case.

Paul Rice, a short man, his hair greying on top of his youthful face, was the Queen's Counsel who acted for Dr Millhouse. He countered the arguments of Tony Bishop and argued that speculation was not sufficient in this case. He forcefully argued that the prosecution had not proved its case and commented how Dr Millhouse gave evidence on oath and he survived the cross-examination without any problems. He argued that it was dangerous for the jury to accept circumstantial evidence and mentioned several cases in which a convicted person was later found to be innocent. His arguments would have caused some of the jury to be concerned about the evidence. But the real crunch for Lee Haddon came when Justice Mohr summed up on 9 October 1980.

Justice Mohr slated the prosecution's case during a talk to the jury lasting just under two hours. He strongly pointed out to the jury that suspicions and innuendoes were not enough. Any blood in the bathroom could not be shown to have belonged to Neil Muir. Items such as the clothesline and garbage bags were common items that could have been used by anyone. Although there were fibres on the Bandaid, the judge speculated that the Bandaid couldhave got into Neil Muir's garbage bag from the Port River and the fibres may have come from another rug. Other evidence did link Neil Muir with the doctor; they had an association but the doctor's denials occurred because he was concerned about his supply of drugs to addicts.

He asked the jury to be concerned only with facts. He also made the point that lies told by the doctor do not indicate a guilty conscience in relation to murder. He said that the lies may have been told for other reasons and noted that Millhouse had told the jury in his evidence that he was worried about losing his practice. Justice Mohr said that statements by the prosecution about sex between Dr Millhouse and Neil Muir were just speculation and had not been proven. In fact, he said the prosecution had proved no motive. The judge summed up and the jury of seven women and five men left the courtroom. They returned seventy-five minutes later.

'Not Guilty,' the foreman said.

It would have been a very brave jury that convicted Dr Millhouse after the summing up from Justice Mohr. Dr Millhouse's mother and father were naturally very relieved at the verdict. They left the courtroom and returned to Mount Gambier with their son.

Chapter 5

Serial Killers

The evidence did not show that Dr Millhouse killed Neil Muir. The police psychologist, Milton Kelly, gave one view: the killer was someone who knew Neil Muir and could have mutilated him to punish him for real or imagined insults. This theory fitted with the views of Lee Haddon. Doctor Millhouse and Neil Muir may have had a falling out but there was no evidence to suggest this happened. In fact, many of the statements obtained by the police indicated that he was more likely not to have killed Neil. Witnesses said that Dr Millhouse was not violent. In fact, he was a weak man who would not start a fight.

I accepted Lee's opinion about Dr Millhouse. He was an experienced detective and he knew the intimate details of the case. I only knew what I had read in the papers and the story from Lee. But something happened that caused me to reconsider my views on the case.

I was present in the Major Crime offices on the fourth floor of the Angas Street police building after Richard Kelvin was found. The squad office followed the open space layout of many modern office buildings, with the bosses in their own rooms at the end of the open spaces. The room was filled with older-style wooden desks with three drawers on the right-hand side, running down to the floor. Wire stacker baskets contained smaller amounts of paperwork which did not belong in the lever-arch files containing the statements from witnesses who could tell things to the police about murder investigations. These folders were kept on the desk if they were active files or in a storeroom if they were older files.

I was sitting at my desk working on some of my files relating to another killing, which happened at Coober Pedy. Glen Lawrie and I had been travelling to the outback town to investigate the killing, which had been witnessed by the local detective.

Trevor Kipling and Lee Haddon were talking about the Muir murder shortly after Richard Kelvin had been found.

'I don't think Millhouse did Muir. I think the same people have killed the lot,' Trevor said.

'No, that's not right. Millhouse did Muir,' Lee said as a tenseness started to set around his lips.

'I bet you that the same people did the lot and Millhouse is not the one,' Trevor said softly, but his words were heard by some of us in the office.

Lee's face flushed and reddened. 'Look, I should know. I arrested him. He did it, I'm telling you,' Lee said in a voice that was pitching slightly higher as his frustration and anger rose from the suggestion that his assessment about Millhouse may have been wrong.

Lee was a sergeant and an experienced detective while Trevor was a senior constable, so Trevor was criticising a senior officer. Both had strong life experiences to back their judgement as police officers. Trevor liked to get out bush or go fishing and had been a country policeman in his earlier days. Lee, on the other hand, preferred the city life but had experience serving as a United Nations peacekeeper in Cyprus when State police were sent to that island as part of a much larger peacekeeping force to stop the fighting between the Greek and Turkish Cypriots.

I'm staying out of this one, I thought.

Trevor was questioning Lee's decision to arrest Peter Millhouse. At that time I didn't know enough about the earlier murders of the young men to have a view as to who was right; but if Trevor was right, then we were looking at Milton Kelly's alternative hypothesis that Neil Muir did not know his murderer and was sought out by his killer to relieve sexual and sadistic needs. This fitted with Trevor Kipling's idea that the killer was a stranger to Neil Muir. Doctor Millhouse wasn't involved. We were looking for at least one serial killer and, if more than one person were involved, then we were looking for serial killers who were preying on young men. We could be looking for serial killers who had abducted, abused and murdered five boys.

We had thought for some time that more than one person was involved in the murders. We had found more people that had heard Richard Kelvin's abduction. A woman in Ward Street heard two voices — an argument at about the time Richard was snatched. One of the voices sounded higher pitched. There were car doors slamming and a car taking off. She thought the noises came from behind her house, where a laneway runs between Margaret and Murray Streets. Another woman living in apartments on Ward Street had her windows open and heard a yell and screeching of tyres like someone trying to run someone over. She thought that there were three or four involved and perhaps heard a female voice. A young couple in Margaret Street heard a shout and people talking. They thought they heard two male voices and a noisy car. Finally, the guy who was ill in bed was a security guard and he was interested in cars. Because of his interest in cars and occupation, he liked to pick the type of car when he heard exhaust noises. There are differences in sound, which allow a person to guess whether the car is a Holden or Falcon with a four cylinder, six cylinder or even a V–8 motor in it.

The security guard heard the cries for help, a whole lot of voices, car doors banging and a car that sounded like a Holden with a bad muffler driving off. Four different lots of people heard the abduction. The first witness thought it was about 5.30 that Sunday evening but all the rest said it was about 6.20 and that they knew the time because they were carrying out a set routine with a baby or they were watching the news.

We thought more than one person was involved with the abductions. This confirmed in our minds that more than one person grabbed Richard Kelvin. More likely than not more than one person was involved in the others. All of the boys were tall and reasonably well built. The only exception was Neil Muir. He was smaller. However, to cut up and dispose of Neil Muir in the way it was done probably meant more than one person although we couldn't be sure.

We were looking for males, as men commit most murders. If there are more than two people involved, experts suggest that there would be a dominant person who has influence over more passive members of the group. When a group is involved, there is a bond because of a shared understanding and a common agreement about purpose.

The high-pitched voice was interesting. We knew that Richard Kelvin's voice had broken and it was a deep male voice even when he raised his voice when he was happy and excited.

Could a woman be involved? we wondered.

The possibility of a woman being involved was a little different. Women have killed and will kill again but generally they kill their partners. Women have been involved in sexual and sadistic crimes of abuse but if any women were involved, then it would be unlikely that one would be the leader of the pack.

If the murders were connected, we were looking for serial killers. Some people refer to serial killings and use the words 'mass killings'. Mass killing is used in the same context as serial killing but the two are different. Serial killings are murders committed at different times. Serial killers have an emotional cycle in which they kill, cool off and then kill again, whereas mass killings are the killing of more than one person as part of one incident. The killings at Jonestown of the religious followers of the Jones cult were mass killings. When a man kills his large family that is a mass killing. There is a commonality with the victims and it is one event. During World War II, it was Jews or members of other minority groups that were slaughtered. These are both examples of mass killings because there was no emotional cycle involved. They were mass killings for a political purpose.

Serial killers are skilful and accomplished in what they do. They cloak themselves in a normal way of life to hide their activities. They don't flee the scene of the crime as many killers do. Many killers will flee and go interstate or may even leave the country but not serial killers. They continue with their daily lives. Their behaviour, on the surface, is perfectly normal. That is not to say serial killers won't move around but their travelling is to find other victims. They are not fleeing from possible capture. If serial killings stop, then there has been a significant event, which brings a halt to the murder spree: the killer has committed suicide, he has moved to another location and is killing there or he has been imprisoned. The Truro murders stopped because the leader of the duo, Christopher Worrell, was killed in a car crash.

Serial killers are generally white, heterosexual men in their twenties or thirties. They tend to target women and children who are the same race as them. Prostitutes, homeless people and hitchhikers are often their victims. If the serial killer is homosexual, then pleasure comes from pursuing young boys and gay men. If the serial killer is a woman, then she will kill her husband, lover or family members. Medical professionals, such as 'Dr Death' in

England, will kill their patients, who include babies, elderly men and women. Nurses who are serial killers will prey on the same type of people.

Serial killers look like normal people. That's how they are able to ply their trade. People are not always who you think they are. I remember snooping outside the window of a drug dealer one hot night when I was in the Drug Squad. The window was open and the dealer was talking to his girlfriend, a nurse, who used heroin. They were talking about drugs.

'I wonder what people would think, if they knew I was using,' she said.

She looked like a normal person, acted like a normal person, worked as a nurse looking after people but was a heroin user. She hadn't become a junkie. Her appearance and body shape had not deteriorated. Many people think that drug use results in an addiction and a downward spiral with physical wellbeing deteriorating, as was happening to Neil Muir. However, many users do not become emaciated but keep their healthy appearance just as many alcoholics do. They look normal. Serial killers can look normal. They can be charming individuals.

As children, serial killers may have been chronic bed wetters as a result of domestic violence in their household. Also, there may be an addiction to either alcohol or drugs or both. Most serial killers possess average or above average intelligence, with some having superior intelligence.

With these murders our offenders were most likely to be homosexuals — violent ones at that — who had the ability to move about Adelaide without bringing attention to themselves. The generally mentioned figure is that ten per cent of the population is homosexual. Given that, with South Australia's population of about 1.5 million, then 150,000 people in South Australia are homosexual. If fifty per cent of them are males, then 75,000 men in South Australia are homosexual. Actually, no-one knows the exact figures but, whatever the numbers are, it is still likely to be in the thousands of men. Even if one per cent of males are homosexual, then we had 7,500 men to consider. How many of that number are violent? Obviously, checking criminal records for crimes of violence involving homosexuals was one way but that would be an extremely laborious task. Police records were still being computerised in 1983 and even when they were the ability to work the database was limited.

The homicidal rampages of serial killers are thought to have a sexual component. The murders are part of an elaborate fantasy that climaxes at the time of killing. Authors believe that the killing becomes a part of a ritual, and has been described as an 'emotional sexual orgasm — the explosion of power'.

Serial killers are sadistic. They murder and then 'cool off' before their need to satisfy their fantasies builds again. This explained the now-regular style of murders. There were two in 1979 — Alan Barnes and Neil Muir disappeared within two months of one another. Then, there was a longer period of two years before Peter Stogneff disappeared. Then a gap of five months before Mark Langley and then a gap of nearly eighteen months before Richard Kelvin was snatched.

Serial killers obtain satisfaction from activities such as cannibalism, necrophilia (sex with a corpse) and keeping souvenirs of their work — trophies that celebrate their activities. Were the body parts of Neil Muir that were missing, the testicle for instance, kept as trophies? Three theories were possible. One theory suggested that the testicle was eaten as a part of a cannibalistic ceremony to celebrate the occasion or the testicle was simply lost during the butchering of Neil Muir. A third theory suggested that the items were taken as trophies to remind the murderers of the occasion. The silver necklace and ingot with Mark Langley's star-sign on it, and his blue satin shirt, were missing. Were they kept as trophies to gloat over or the items merely disposed of because they were marked or bloodied? We couldn't discount any of these possibilities and the existence of different theories made the investigation harder to narrow down and allow us to focus our efforts in one direction.

Some authors say that serial killers are fascinated with the remains of their crimes and may visit their victims' graves and even attend their funerals. Trevor asked me to attend the funeral of Peter Stogneff early in 1983. He was buried at Cheltenham Cemetery, which lies adjacent to Port Road. The large plot of land extends from Port Road almost to the railway line that bisects Cheltenham Parade. The flat burial ground is divided by three walkways that cross and separate the gravestones. Distant relatives of mine are buried there and I find the cemetery uninspiring. However, there were two reasons to attend the funeral. There was the remote chance that someone other than the kindred family and friends were hanging around that day but also I went to represent police and support the Stogneff family.

I stood at the back watching the service and looking around for anything unusual. Nothing extraordinary happened on the day but I realised my limitations a week later. An envelope arrived at Major Crime addressed to me. I opened it and found a picture of me at the Cheltenham Cemetery looking very serious and trying to pick anything unusual. I was photographed by police surveillance who were also sent to the funeral service by Trevor — so much for my observation skills! On reflection, I think that I only had an average score for observation from my test during my detective training course.

Both Trevor and I went to Centennial Park to the funeral of Richard Kelvin on 9 September 1983. We stayed in the background as much as possible. I never asked Trevor about surveillance but I knew the police officers in the plain van would be there somewhere in the distance with their binoculars and telescopic camera lens.

Experts describe serial killers as: psychopathic sexual sadists, who torture and kill for pleasure; crime-spree killers; organised crime members of the Mafia or street gangs; custodial poisoners; or asphyxiators such as doctors and nurses who have control over people. The fifth category is psychotics whose crimes result from psychotic delusions. Terrorists, who are politically motivated, could be added to this list.

Other experts separate the crime-spree rapist who kills and the sexual sadist. They distinguish between killers who murder after a sexual assault to stop the victim identifying the killer from those who kill for pleasure. A hedonistic killer may kill for sexual pleasure or the excitement of a novel experience while those seeking power and control, where domination over the victim is important, want any sexual activity as part of that domination. All of these factors were considerations we had to take into account.

The sexual sadist kills as a part of his sexual gratification and this category of serial killer has been written about the most. Christopher Worrell of Truro infamy initially killed to stop a victim identifying him to police but, most likely, he moved to killing for pleasure as he picked up more girls, even though the secondary aspect of identification would have been in the back of his sick mind. While some academics put people in boxes, in real life it is never that simple.

There are five stages to a serial murder. They are:

1. Fantasy;
2. Stalking;
3. Abduction;
4. Killing; and
5. Disposal.

The fantasy stage occurs as the killer starts thinking about killing. He fantasises about what he is going to do and the intensity of the deviant mind-games increases to the stage when stalking of a victim commences. Once a victim is found, that person is stalked and then abducted before being killed and disposed of as an object which is no longer useful.

Other experts add three phases to the process of serial killing. Between the stalking of a victim and the abduction there may be a wooing phase, in which the victim is seduced or their defences are lowered. Richard Kelvin was abducted but what about the other boys? Were they forced into a car or were they seduced into a situation where they could be controlled?

In the Totem Phase, the preservation of the intensity of the murder is maintained by the keeping of bits of a body. Genitals are cut off or even limbs severed. The Totem Phase reminded me of what I already knew about the keeping of trophies and maybe even the missing lower legs of Peter Stogneff fitted into this idea. Peter's lower limbs, however, may have been lost to a fox fossicking for food. And, finally, after the disposal of the body, there may be bouts of depression before depraved fantasies start to build again. Experts have presented eight phases of serial killers that police need to consider:

1. Fantasy;
2. Stalking;
3. Wooing;
4. Abduction;
5. Killing;
6. Trophies;
7. Disposal; and
8. Depression.

Also, serial killers have been classified by whether they are organised or disorganised offenders, based on the crime scene. Offenders may leave a crime scene tidy, reflecting that they are organised and planning is involved. The organised offender may use restraints to control and have power over the victim, commit sexual acts with live victims and use a vehicle. The disorganised offender is likely to leave evidence at the scene, perform sexual acts with the victim after death and not use a vehicle. We did not have crime scenes where the boys were killed. This indicated that we were looking for someone who was organised, methodical and had access to a vehicle. We could not ignore the possibility that the killers had just moved to Adelaide and were now part of the community. They could move on just as quickly, or they could be established members of Adelaide's society of one million people.

The interesting thing about understanding serial killers is trying to find out why a person is selected as the next victim. Is it something about their smile, their clothes, their hair or the way that they carry themselves? I was sure that the killers would have seen Richard Kelvin wearing that dog collar around his neck when he was at the bus stop in O'Connell Street just before he was abducted. If our serial killer was a homosexual sexual sadist then fantasies involving Richard and the dog collar could have been a real turn on. On top of all this, Trevor had spoken to the police psychologists and they said that if we had a serial killer or killers stalking the streets, then they would kill again.

While Lee Haddon had worked in the belief that Neil Muir had been murdered by someone close to him, Trevor worked in the belief that a stranger to the victims was involved. He worked on the homosexual angle. Trevor believed the killer was a violent homosexual who picked up Mark Langley after he walked off from his friend's car. As the police psychologist, Ray Dowd, indicated with Neil Muir, the killer might be a homosexual who had strong sexual fantasies.

When Trevor and Paul Maddern were working together on the Mark Langley case, they were spending a lot of time on the banks of the River Torrens near where Mark went missing. Trevor and Paul went to areas which we learned later were called 'the beats'. Homosexuals used the beats as meeting places.

The beats were areas around the city of Adelaide where men would meet with the idea of having sex, to relieve tension or satisfy their fantasies. Invariably, the beats were near toilets where sex could be practised. If the police spoke to them about their presence in the area, the men could honestly say they were going to the toilet.

'Number One beat' was underneath the King William Road Bridge along the River Torrens to the bridge near the Adelaide Zoo. King William Road is an extension of King William Street, which stretches through the centre of Adelaide. The wide street splits the city into two and, as it heads north, the road crosses the River Torrens over an attractive, wide concrete bridge. The road then runs past Adelaide Oval and curves into North Adelaide, where Adelaide's gentry live, specialist doctors practise and Rob and Betteanne Kelvin lived. Mark Langley disappeared near Number One beat.

The toilets built behind Jolly's Boathouse, which is now a popular Adelaide restaurant overlooking the still waters of the river, were part of the beat. The lively chatter from the patrons of the restaurant changes to quieter words in the darkness of the night amongst the trees and shrubs of the riverbank. Homosexuals come together in the vicinity of the boathouse, meeting on the grassy banks or the lower or higher walking path. The paths, supported by free-stone retaining walls, have occasional seats set back in recesses, allowing quiet meetings to happen.

Other beats exist around the city of Adelaide. Another popular one is at Veale Gardens off South Terrace, Adelaide. An access road runs behind the gardens. It stretches 500 metres to the restaurant, 'Pavilion on the Park', which is hidden from the city by the Glenelg tramline and shrubs between the restaurant and King William Street. Half-way along the access road there are more toilets, which are the focal point of the beat.

The beat on Unley Road was between South Terrace and Greenhill Road. The shabby toilets have since been demolished because of concerns about contact between the beat's visitors and those using the BMX bike track that had been built just south of the toilets. The planners thought they were doing a good job. The kids needed a bike track, there was room in the parklands and there were toilets nearby for the kids to use. The planners obviously didn't know that the area was a beat. Their understanding changed over the years and the toilets were bulldozed.

Another beat was on Glen Osmond Road also between South Terrace and Greenhill Road. Picnickers sit on the soft grass and use the playground and barbecue facilities during the day. At night, the area is used for other reasons. Homosexuals who want to met other men go there, including married men who seek pleasure and excitement different from that provided by their wives — and, just perhaps, people visiting the beats were serial killers.

Chapter 6

New Leads

By this stage of the investigation we had some police with different viewpoints, others who were out and about at all hours of the night in some pretty unsavoury places but we only had a few other leads — nothing concrete. What we needed was one crucial piece in the jigsaw that could open our eyes to the solution.

Another lead now came into Major Crime. The caller on the telephone was anonymous, as so many are. Obviously, many people want to give information without getting involved. Involvement may mean that the person has to give evidence in court or they may have a grudge against someone and they don't want them to know they are 'dobbing' them into the police. Others want to pass on information that is false.

The call related to a light coloured 1963 EJ Holden sedan driven by two men, Doug and Mark. The male caller said that these two abducted Richard Kelvin. The car was described by the caller as being in good condition, fitted with a tow bar and with two mirrors on the front guards of the car. Thousands of these vehicles were built but, twenty years later, they were becoming scarce. Also, the car was said to be in good condition. That would have been unusual for a car that old. With the details about mirrors and tow bar and with the first names of two men, we were hopeful that someone would know the car and its occupants. We publicised this information with the help of the morning paper, *The Advertiser*, which was distributed throughout the State. The full-page spread on page thirteen called out 'CAN YOU HELP?' 'WANTED' was on the next line with 'REWARD' further down. The full-page spread showed a photo of Richard Kelvin, the distinctive T-shirt he was wearing and two photos of the type of car we were looking for.

Just to organise this type of publicity takes a lot of work. We received calls about people who had those names and vehicles, and who fitted this description but we had no success. This lead led nowhere and, as time passed, Trevor and I became more and more suspicious about the accuracy of the information.

When Trevor and I were investigating the Monteith murders, the killing of an elderly couple near Murray Bridge some time later, we released the description of the offenders' vehicle. The vehicle used was quite common. It was a white Holden one-ton ute. Again, there were thousands around.

However, the large storage box on the back of the vehicle immediately behind the cabin was unusual. It was large and had a sloping lid. We received calls about that vehicle almost straight away and we arrested one of the murderers within two days of the information being released. The vehicle that was heard during the abduction of Richard Kelvin was believed to have a loud exhaust. This didn't fit with a vehicle being in good condition. We were starting to wonder — was it a false lead?

Another telephone caller suggested that Richard Kelvin had been used as a real-life player in a video. What the caller was talking about were 'snuff movies': films that show a person actually being murdered. We had discussed the possibility of snuff movies and speculation was rife that this type of film existed, although no one actually had seen one. We contemplated whether or not the boys were filmed as real-life actors in a hideous play of death and abuse. We could not ignore the possibility. Investigations were made in that direction.

Enormous difficulties surrounded this type of enquiry. Films can appear to be so real that a viewer cannot tell whether or not the person was actually killed or it was an act. Therefore, snuff movies might not even exist and people who see them only think that they are seeing a real movie. Also, we believed that the control of real snuff movies is kept so tight that only those in the inner sanctum of groups interested in this type of ghoulish film get to see it. If such films exist, they would be smuggled into the country and not openly distributed. They could easily come in the video jacket of another film. The checking of individual videos does not happen, as Customs has a major focus towards drugs, weapons and other illegal items. Also, snuff films could be imported via the internet. We did not find any snuff movies, although I am sure that there would be some out there in this crazy world of ours.

More than likely any snuff movie would have been kept by the serial killers for their own enjoyment — to relive the moment. The Investigation Support Unit of the FBI in America can tell of cases in which the cries of victims were tape-recorded and the deaths of others were filmed. However, the films and tapes were not sold or copied. They were kept for the killers' own pleasure and recall.

Another video we tried to locate was supposedly called *Black and Blue*. The film was supposed to show a young boy wearing a dog collar around his neck being led around on all fours. We weren't sure whether it related to a snuff movie or it was a video that related to 'S & M' — sadistic and masochistic behaviour. If a video showing this type of behaviour was around, it could have all sorts of implications. Such a video would excite people with those tendencies toward having power and control over others. If we could find the video, we might find the people who were into this type of behaviour. If a film of this type came into the country legally and had an R-rating, then the video shops renting might have some records of the people who hired it. However, a check with film distributors, censors and video outlets produced no results. We were back to square one with that lead and more time was lost. But we couldn't ignore the possibility of snuff movies and *Black and Blue*. When Richard Kelvin wore that dog collar to the bus stop it would have produced a second glance from most people and perhaps an excited stare from those into power and control.

A disgusting video that we did find was titled *Fist Fuckers of America*, which graphically showed men inserting their whole hands into the anuses of other men. The film showed what some people will do and just what some people are into. Also, it showed just how much the muscles of the anus would stretch. A man who regularly experienced anal sex could have an enlarged anus but we had a different situation here and the experts were still talking about a bottle being used on the local victims, although we couldn't discount other possibilities.

The search for the elusive caravan, the EJ Holden sedan, the investigation and trial of Dr Millhouse, as well as the search for snuff and S & M movies were all potentially important leads that consumed a lot of time and effort. They were just some of the leads that were investigated that did not provide any more clues to help solve the murders. They led nowhere, but one benefit from carrying out these enquiries would be to help negate defence efforts to confuse a jury if we were successful. We could provide answers to defence suggestions that the boys may have been used in snuff movies in any trial. I have been describing some of the efforts of the detectives but there was just as much effort put into the examination of the boys' bodies. The efforts of the forensic scientists were just as time consuming.

Crime scene examiner Ivan Sarvas, had lifted Richard Kelvin's body onto a stretcher with the pathologist, Ross James, and placed him in the coroner's van. At the mortuary,

Des Phillips supervised the removal of his clothing and placed it into paper bags, rather than plastic, so it could breathe and not go mouldy. He marked the clothes with the name 'R. KELVIN' and put the date and name of the items on the bag. Des took the bags for examination but he had to dry the body fluids from the clothes before he could properly examine those. The clothes were placed in a drying cabinet which has a stainless steel base. The exhaust fan at the top of the cabinet draws air over the clothes and they dry naturally. Both officers recorded on their own files the time when the items changed hands. Ivan and Des were meticulous with their work, which later received strong praise from the Crown prosecutor.

Des was looking for paint, hair and fibres on the clothing that did not come from Richard's home environment. He was looking for 'trace evidence'. The words are derived from Lochard, a scientist, who stated that every contact between two objects leaves a trace of that contact. Trace of that contact can be shown by the evidence left behind.

Other crime scene examiners did the same for the clothing of Alan Barnes and Mark Langley. They did the examination of the clothing by vacuuming it inside and out when it was dry. They used tape lifts to remove foreign objects from the clothes. Clear adhesive tape is placed on the garments and then lifted off. Obviously, a lot of tape is used to cover all of the clothing. It has to be done for each different piece of clothing and for different sections of it. 'Tape lifts' and the vacuuming are done both outside and inside the clothing. But first the tape has to be visually examined to make sure that no foreign objects are adhering to it — if that was the case, then the evidence would be contaminated.

If hair was found on some clothing then the location at which the hair was found on the clothing becomes important. If head hair was found on the shoulders of a shirt, then, naturally, the first thing to check would be the hair of the person who was wearing the shirt. Most likely it would have come from the person wearing the shirt. If the hair was on underpants, then a comparison of pubic hair would be made first to determine whether or not it came from that location. Naturally, if the hair did not belong to the person wearing the clothing we then asked: 'Where did it come from? Whose hair was it?'

Trace evidence was found on the right palm of Alan Barnes. It was a paint chip but it was similar to the yellow paint from the railing of the bridge over the reservoir. Also, on his clothes, he had red, blue, yellow and white spray paint. There was vegetation on his clothes, which consisted of minute traces of a common weed, a type of bracken, moss, thistle weed and a rare gum nut. This type of nut was only found in the Adelaide Hills north of the River Torrens and does not grow 1.5 kilometres north of Williamstown. Probably, it came from the nearby area. Silt was in Barnes' clothing. However, as mica was not present in the silt, the Warren, South Para, Millbrook Reservoirs in the Adelaide Hills and the Barossa Reservoir were discounted. We worked on the possibility that he had been washed and cleaned in a dam or catchment area in the Adelaide Hills where the vegetation was found. We wondered whether or not the caravan that might have kept Richard Kelvin captive was near that dam or catchment area. We didn't check around the location where Mark Langley was found as it was south of the River Torrens but we checked various locations around the airstrip and the Kersbrook/Williamstown area. We were trying to find a place where Alan Barnes could have been held and subsequently washed.

Des Carroll, a tall police officer who now works in the Forensic Science Centre, came with us. He was young and educated. He had gone to university to study botany to help with the identification of cannabis plants, which were becoming more and more prevalent during those years. Now, his training in botany was being used to investigate murders. One possible location where Alan Barnes could have been cleaned was a small roadside park about four kilometres south of Williamstown on the road between Kersbrook and Williamstown. The roadside park looked like it had been created when the new bitumen road had been straightened, allowing the bend to become a roadside park. All the relevant plants were present, including specimens of the rare gum tree. Water was held in low-lying sections of the roadside area, washed from the road and drained from the slopes of the adjacent paddocks. Alan Barnes or his clothes or both could have been washed in the pool of water before he was thrown from the bridge. Why would that have happened? Why would the murderers have wanted to wash the boys?

The bodily fluids from the decomposition of Mark Langley caused problems in obtaining much trace material from his clothes but small quantities of various metals were found on the clothing. As he worked as a plumber, they were explained away. No clothes were found on Neil Muir and Peter Stogneff. Crime scene examiners Ivan Sarvas and John Parkes sifted the area around where Peter was found but if his clothes were dumped with him then the fire destroyed any sign of them.

Des Phillips' tape lifts from the clothes of Richard Kelvin produced a great deal of trace material. There were many fibres foreign to the clothes and he painstakingly recorded their locations before separating them. The foreign fibres were separated into different colours. He separated blue, turquoise, purple, orange, yellow, black, brown, red and green fibres before handing them to Sandra Mattner, forensic scientist, from the Chemistry Section for analysis. Hairs, not belonging to Richard, were recovered and handed to Dr Harry Harding of the Forensic Biology Laboratory.

These materials had to be examined and those analyses are often slow, painstaking tasks. But as the months passed we learned the importance of the fibres and hairs. Examinations of Richard's organs also produced clues, and it was these that could be used much sooner.

Things happen at post-mortem examinations which I have not explained previously. Obviously, the body is examined to note and record the physical injuries but there is an examination of the brain and internal organs as well. Examination and tests conducted on different parts of the body help determine the cause of death, which proves whether a killing is deliberate or accidental — obviously, an essential thing to prove in a murder case.

To examine the brain, a scalpel is used to cut across the top of the head and the scalp is pulled to the front and the back, exposing the top of the skull, which is cut using a Hall oscillating saw. The circular blade oscillates rather than rotates. Oscillations of the blade cut bone but do not damage soft tissue. If anyone has had a cast on a broken bone, a saw is used to cut plaster from the limb. The saw does not cut the skin and, in a post-mortem, the saw allows the top of the head to be lifted, exposing the brain and fluid around the brain without it being damaged. The brain is removed and sliced by the pathologist to check for obvious damage. Bruising to the brain and brain stem indicate a knock to the head.

Samples from the body's organs, blood and urine are taken for examination for any sign of drugs in the system, while there is also checking for damage to ligatures and bruising to the skin and tissues surrounding the throat as well as checks for evidence of strangulation.

The skin over the chest is cut down the line of the breastbone, exposing the ribs, which are cut in line with each side of the body with implements that look like large secateurs to allow access to the organs of the body. Samples from the organs and blood from the abdominal cavity are taken for examination and testing to determine whether or not drugs were in the body and whether or not death may have been caused naturally. Although people may be horribly injured, sometimes death may have been caused by a heart attack or stroke. If this is the case, then proving murder is complicated as the prosecutor then has to show that the heart attack was directly a result of the injury that the assailant caused — a very difficult task.

The post-mortem examination of Alan Barnes revealed that he had most likely been killed on the Friday, a relatively short time prior to his dumping on the Saturday. The absence of decay of his body also indicated this to the pathologist. He had been eating and drinking just before he was killed — about two to three hours — as something similar to a fried egg was in his stomach. Also, he had been drinking, as his blood alcohol level was high at 0.19% compared with the driving limit of 0.05%. As well as alcohol, tests revealed that he had trichloroethanol in his blood, liver and stomach. Trichloroethanol is produced when chloral hydrate metabolises in the body. Chloral hydrate is the active ingredient of Noctec. Noctec is a drug in capsule form. It is a sedative and hypnotic drug used since the 1970s for treating sufferers of insomnia. The drug allays anxiety and induces sleep but the taking of the drug can become habit forming. Alcohol increases its potency. That made things interesting. Here we were with Alan Barnes full of booze with a knock-out drug in him.

We believed he was experimenting with drugs but was the food given to him to hide the fact he was being given drugs or did he take them voluntarily? Either scenario was a possibility, I speculated.

With the other bodies, we were also left with little to go on but speculation. The internal organs of Neil Muir were missing but the brain was still present in the skull. Without the stomach and organs, the police were unable to test for the presence of drugs. We wondered whether or not the stomach was taken out to remove the presence of any drugs or food in the stomach that might have given us a lead. But that was pure speculation. The cutting up of Neil Muir, which could only be described as a complete mutilation, was still a mystery.

The same situation applied to Peter Stogneff. No examination of the organs and brain was possible with Peter Stogneff because only his skeleton was found.

Mark Langley had a stitched incision in his abdomen. The thread used to stitch the wound and the Johnson & Johnson tape provided some evidence to go on. John Woite, the other sergeant on Glen Lawrie's team, spoke to the media after checking with different companies about which one made it. When he found that it was Johnson & Johnson tape, he showed a container of the tape to the media and asked for publicity on it, trying to stir somebody's memory or conscience — requesting information from members of the public. Obviously, publicity about the tape also allows murderers to get rid of their supplies of their tape but we were desperate for leads and we had to take a chance.

Food was also in the stomach of Mark Langley. It was corn but because he was killed fairly soon after he disappeared and because corn was a favourite food of his, we felt that the food came from the party that he went to on the Saturday night or was already present in his stomach.

Richard Kelvin also had undigested food in his stomach, but it was hard for the scientists to determine the type. Chris Pearman, another police botanist, believed that he might have eaten an apple before he was killed. He also thought there were starches in his stomach and later tests showed those starches most likely came from cornflakes.

At the same time tests were being conducted by the chemists of the Forensic Science Centre. The initial tests were conducted on the Monday and Tuesday after Richard was found. On Wednesday, 27 July 1983, three days after Richard was found, we were called to the Forensic Science Centre. Bob Lokan, chief chemist, spoke with us.

'We're getting indications of drugs in Richard Kelvin.'

'What sort?' Trevor asked.

'We're still doing tests but it looks like Richard Kelvin was given chloral hydrate, just like Alan Barnes.'

'Can you check with his parents to see if he was taking any drugs?'

The remains of the drug Noctec was found in his system — exactly the same as Alan Barnes. More similarities were found and all of these similarities indicated that the same people could be involved. The chemists weren't wasting any time. They knew that these cases were generating an enormous amount of interest and concern.

Trevor and I drove to Rob and Betteanne's home. They had taken time off work after Richard was found. Trevor wanted to tell them about the finding of the drug and to check about Richard's drug use. We didn't believe that he was a drug user but we needed to let his parents know what was happening and also to check whether or not he was taking Noctec and ask about his use of alcohol.

Betteanne confirmed our beliefs. He wasn't taking Noctec or any other drugs but he had tried alcohol, although not to excess to their knowledge — nothing unusual there. He had tried beer but didn't really like it; he may have had a social sip of wine.

The same afternoon we returned to the Forensic Science Centre. One of the chemists, Domenic Vozzo, of the

Toxicology Section, was working on a hunch. In October 1982, a young boy had reported to the Port Adelaide police that he had been picked up by a person in a car and taken to a house somewhere in the Port Adelaide area. At the house, he thought that he had been drugged, because he passed out there. Port Adelaide detectives interviewed the boy and arranged for a doctor to take blood from him so it could be analysed. Initial tests proved negative. Domenic used his initiative and decided to test for other drugs. Methaqualone and dyphenhydramine were found in the boy's blood. Methaqualone and dyphenhydramine were the active ingredients of the drug known as Mandrax, which was a common drug in the 1970s.

Mandrax was used as a substitute for barbiturates, but the drug also was abused. Because of the effects of the methaqualone component of the drug, it was regulated in January 1978 by the Narcotic and Psychotropic Drugs Act. Placing the drug under the Act increased control over it: chemist shops had to record the level of their stocks every three months, and the Central Board of Health had to approve the prescribing of Mandrax to a patient if it continued longer than two months. This regulation was included to try and reduce addiction to the drug. By 1983 stocks of Mandrax in Australia were reducing and the drug was prescribed less and less.

The chemists working on Richard Kelvin remembered the excellent investigatory work by Domenic Vozzo nine months before. They tested for Mandrax and found it present in samples taken from both Richard Kelvin and Mark Langley. Also, with more testing, traces of other drugs were found in the blood of Richard Kelvin.

Richard Kelvin had been given a huge mickey finn. There were four different drugs. The drugs that were used on Richard were Mandrax, Noctec, and a diazepam such as Valium, and 'Amytal'. Amytal was the common name for Amytalobarbitone, which is a long-acting barbiturate used as a sedative and an hypnotic.

Later, we would learn that a fifth drug may have been present in Richard Kelvin's system but the traces were too small to be sure. He may have been given a dose of Rohypnol at some time during his captivity. Rohypnol was a common benzodiazophine of the day. The drug was called 'rollies'. It was a sedative and hypnotic used for the treatment of insomnia. The drug had a popular name because people abused it. Users enjoyed its impact on their bodies. People also enjoyed its impact on other people's bodies and it was obviously used to 'drug' people.

From my time in the Drug Squad, I had heard of Rohypnol tablets being used by men to spike women's drinks. Men would pick up women at discos and offer to buy them drinks. This gave a man the opportunity to pop some rollies in the drink while he was away from an unsuspecting woman. Later, when a woman was affected by the drug, bouncers or barstaff would see the man take the women from the disco but the guy could just say he was taking home his girlfriend who'd had too much to drink. What pub worker would stop someone from taking a friend home who had 'obviously' drunk too much?

Once a woman was out to it, she could be abused in any way.

Now, I had seen the impact of this drug on boys and young men. Rollies were like Noctec but came as a white tablet with a cross on it rather than in a capsule. The drug was quick acting and acted more powerfully when alcohol had been drunk. An overdose of the drug would cause extreme drowsiness and respiratory depression.

All of the drugs found in the boys were 'knock me outs'.

We stood there taking in the news from the forensic chemists. The pieces of the jigsaw were starting to come together. Our suspicions about the murders being linked were being confirmed. With at least three of them, the same people using alcohol and drugs to calm and control their prey most likely killed Alan Barnes, Mark Langley and Richard Kelvin.

Trevor's suspicions look like being right, I thought.

Drugging and abusing people were not new. If you consider alcohol a drug, then men have often used that drug to weaken the defences of women. Men have done it for centuries but the ones Trevor and I were looking for were homosexual deviates who drugged, abused and killed their victims.

We were very secretive about the knowledge we gained from the result of the post-mortem examinations. We had released plenty of information about the sticking plaster on Mark Langley, the suspected vehicle and the possibility of a caravan being used for Richard Kelvin. But we didn't have to release this information and decided that was the best play at this stage. We now had some evidence which we could use to check stories or to prove someone might be involved in the murders. We weren't going to give them an opportunity to get rid of any hidden drugs.

The same afternoon we found out about the drugs, Trevor and I drove the short distance from the Angas Street police building to the Health Commission building on the north-eastern corner of Rundle Mall and Pultney Street. Things were starting to speed up. We had something new to work with and we couldn't afford to let the trail go cold. Richard's body had been found, the chemists had shown a scientific link between three of the murders and they did it in record time. We weren't about to slacken up.

The ordinary looking eight-storey building we headed for housed the Bank of South Australia on the ground floor and Health Commission records upstairs. They kept copies of prescriptions for restricted drugs. We wanted to check their records about the prescribing of Mandrax.

We went to the front counter and introduced ourselves to the office staff, who were waiting for us. Trevor had previously rung and told them what we were looking for. They helpfully showed us into the room containing the files, pointed in the direction where the prescriptions for Mandrax were stored and left us to it. We pulled out a couple of the drawers and each took one and we started thumbing our way through individual scripts.

What a pain, doing this, I thought. Going through drawers containing thousands of scripts was hardly exciting detective work. When I was seconded to the Major Crime Squad for the Truro murders, I was a junior detective and for the first month two of us went through missing person files — one at a time. For one month I was just checking files but later I got out on the road and obtained statements from people who were on the periphery of the case. Now, here were the two primary team detectives checking files. I had a sense of *déjà vu* but it had to be done and it was our best lead.

We had been checking the Mandrax scripts for a very short time — only about one hour.

'Look at this!' Trevor said excitedly.

I looked blankly at a script for Mandrax with a name written on the top: B. von Einem. The name didn't mean anything to me. I had been on the case for seven weeks but I hadn't had time to read the other boys' murder files. The finding of the drugs in the boys was our first big break. I quickly learned this was our second.

Chapter 7

Bevan Spencer von Einem

Bevan Spencer von Einem first became known to police in 1972, not because he had committed any crime, but because he was a good Samaritan.

On the night of 10 May 1972, almost ten years before Mark Langley disappeared from near the Torrens River, Dr George Duncan, a university lecturer, was thrown into the river by a group of men. Later, the group was alleged to have been police officers from the Vice Squad of the South Australian police. Another Vice Squad officer blew the whistle on his fellow officers and said that police were down at the Torrens to throw homosexuals into the river. Vice officers were required to police homosexual behaviour, which was still against the law at the time. Of course, they visited the homosexual haunts and the beats. It was alleged that it was a common practice of Vice Squad police at the time was to throw homosexuals into the river rather than properly police homosexuality. Tragically, Dr Duncan was thrown into the dark waters of the river and drowned. Later, two former police officers were charged with manslaughter but they were found not guilty.

What is not commonly known is that a second man was thrown into the river that night and saw the doctor drowning. But he could not help because his leg had been broken when he was thrown in. He had to struggle from the river, fearful that the group of men, who had thrown him in, might come back. He struggled up the bank of the river to Victoria Terrace, which runs alongside the river between it and the military barracks on the other side. He did find help, however; the person who took him to the Royal Adelaide Hospital was Bevan Spencer von Einem.

Obviously, this behaviour did not make von Einem a suspect for murder — far from it. His actions made him less likely to be a murderer but Trevor knew more. He had read the other murder files.

A caller to the police, who later would become well known to me, nominated von Einem as a person involved in the murder of Alan Barnes. He telephoned on Tuesday, 26 June 1979, two days after Alan's body was found. Other than that phone call, there was nothing to link von Einem with the murder. Rod Hunter, a senior detective, interviewed him. Rod was a big man and a very experienced homicide detective. He could normally 'smell a rat' and pick if someone was lying. When he spoke to von Einem on 2 September 1979, nearly three years before Richard Kelvin was snatched, von Einem denied knowing Alan Barnes and having anything to do with his death. Von Einem did say he was a homosexual, volunteering that he had visited the Mars Bar, a gay and lesbian dance club in Gouger Street. Von Einem also gave information to Rod Hunter about another of the missing boys.

'Are you investigating the death of Neil Muir?' von Einem asked.

'I'm not but some members of our squad are,' Rod Hunter replied. 'Why is that?'

'I know Neil Muir. I saw him last Saturday night.'

'Do you mean that you saw him last night?' Rod tested him to see if he knew what he was talking about.

'No, the Saturday before.'

'Where and when did you see him that night?'

'I left home at 9 p.m. and drove into the city to the Duke of York. Neil was there drinking with a man. I left about 10 p.m. and went to the "Buck". Neil wanted me to go to the Lord Melbourne with him but I had promised to meet someone at the Buckingham Arms.'

'Was Neil Muir a homosexual?'

'Yes.'

'How do you know that?'

'About four years ago I went to bed with him.'

'Who did you promise to meet at the Buckingham Arms?'

'Miss S. I dropped S there on my way to town and told her that if she didn't come into the Duke of York by 10 p.m., I would come back for her.'

'Who was Neil Muir drinking with at the Duke of York?'

'I don't know the man but he was introduced as Adam.'

'Did you meet S at the Buck?'

'I drove into the carpark of the Buck and got out of the car. I intended to urinate near a shed. A man came at me with a knife. He said he wanted some "smack". After that I drove home.'

'Were you injured by this man with the knife?'

'Not really, but after I got free all I wanted to do was go home.'

'Did you report this attack to the police?'

'I wanted to, but I talked to my solicitor and then decided not to because of the publicity it might receive.'

'Is there anything else you can tell me about the identity of the man with Muir who was introduced to you as Adam?'

'Only that he was older than Neil. If I find out anything about him, I will let you know.'

'Do you know the identity of the man who attacked you in the carpark of the Buckingham Arms that night?'

'No. I think he might have been Greek or Italian.'

'Did you see Muir again after leaving the Duke of York at about 10 p.m. that night?'

'Yes. He wanted me to go with him to the Lord Melbourne. I wouldn't go but I drove him to the Buck and dropped him there at about 10.15. I didn't see him after that.'

'I will pass this information along to the officers who are handling the Muir enquiry.'

This information was amazing. Von Einem seems to be around every time something happens. On Sunday, 2 September 1979, five days after Neil Muir was found in the river, von Einem said that he had been with Neil Muir on the Saturday night before he was killed! His story was strange. If Neil Muir wanted to go to the Lord Melbourne, why did he take him to the Buckingham Arms Hotel? He would have driven straight past the Lord Melbourne on the way. And that story about being held up with a knife — did that really happen?

Rod Hunter passed this information on to Lee Haddon but by this time Lee was working on the theory that Dr Millhouse was his best lead because he had been dobbed in by two druggies who knew the doctor.

Von Einem's name also came to the attention of police in 1982, very soon after Mark Langley was killed. Major Crime received information during March that year that von Einem picked up boys at the River Torrens and sexually assaulted them. This fitted with Trevor's proposition that a violent homosexual may have picked up Mark Langley.

Detectives John Anderson and Wayne Tonkin were working as a secondary team in Major Crime Squad and they attended von Einem's workplace at Pipeline Supplies of Australia and spoke to von Einem on 25 March 1982, about one month after Mark Langley disappeared. Like the time he was spoken to about Alan Barnes, he told police he was a homosexual and went to the river to meet people and socialise but he denied knowing anything about Mark Langley. He did say that he was out and about that night.

He said that he was drinking at home and left for a drive at about 11 p.m. He said that he took the back streets to miss random breath stations. These actions reminded me of someone moving out at night going for a hunt — looking for prey. I was reminded of the stalking phase of serial killers. Von Einem said that he drove through back streets to the Hackney Hotel, next to the Hackney Bridge, which crosses the River Torrens. He drove to North Adelaide and drove down Melbourne Street and up the hill to O'Connell Street, North Adelaide and bought some fish and chips.

This man is a creature of habit. He said he drove to his work at Pipeline Supplies of Australia at Regency Park and checked the security lights before travelling along Port Road and Hindley Street. He went to the Mars Bar at 1.30 a.m. before leaving at 3.00 a.m. to travel home by the back streets of Stepney — exactly the way Mark Langley would have been trying to go home.

When he was spoken to about Mark Langley, von Einem volunteered a story — just as he did with Rod Hunter, when Rod spoke to him about Alan Barnes. Von Einem said that one week after Mark Langley went missing, he met someone of Lebanese appearance. Von Einem said that this person was held up at the River Torrens by two people with a gun on the night Mark went missing.

Interesting. This was the second hold up von Einem revealed — the first at the Buckingham Arms and now one at the River Torrens. Did these stories mean anything? was the question I now asked myself.

I knew my partner was excited about what we had learned about the drugs and von Einem using Mandrax, a restricted drug, which was found in Richard Kelvin. Von Einem was a homosexual, he hung around the beats and he had been nominated as a person who might have been involved in the murder of Alan Barnes. Also, Noctec had been found in

Alan Barnes and Richard Kelvin. No wonder Trevor was excited. I was excited myself. We had one of our best leads. Trevor was very keen to speak to von Einem.

We drove to the north-eastern suburbs of Adelaide first thing in the morning on Thursday, 28 July 1983, four days after Richard Kelvin had been found. Checks on von Einem's driving licence had him living in the suburb of Paradise. Trevor did not plan a dawn raid. He was not 'gung-ho' like some detectives. He just wanted to go and check out the situation.

We stopped the police car in von Einem's street but not in front of the house. Stopping two houses away was far enough to maintain the element of surprise but also was a routine precaution. Stopping a police car in front of houses where suspects live lets people know we are coming. It gives them time to jump over back fences, or, if a suspect is crazy enough, it gives them time to put a bullet through the window of the police car.

We approached the brush front fence and saw the von Einem house. He lived in a place that best could be described as bland. The three-bedroom home would have been built in the late 1950s or early 1960s, a typical middle-class place made of beige and yellow brick with a reddish-orange concrete tile roof. The unimpressive front yard consisted of a lawn and a driveway with a few scrawny shrubs in front of the bedroom window closest to the front door. The front door was in the middle of the house. A larger lounge window was on the other side of the front door. On that side, a high tin fence joined the house to the side fence, no doubt providing privacy to the rear yard, which I guessed consisted of another lawn and a ubiquitous Australian Hills Hoist. A traditional, rectangular galvanised iron garage was standing at the end of the driveway and another high tin fence joined the house to the garage.

No one driving past the place would have noticed a thing. Its lack of features did not attract attention and the garden was neat and tidy enough not to demand a second look. The most outstanding feature of the house was its ordinariness.

We walked on the lawn that covered the majority of the front yard so our shoes would not crunch on the gravel spread on the driveway. Trevor moved to the front door. I automatically headed to the corner of the house next to the driveway. I was ready to run to the backyard if anyone left in a hurry by the rear door.

Trevor knocked on the door. A few moments passed before a man opened the screen door and stared at Trevor through his glasses. He was taller than my partner by a few centimetres, well proportioned but not muscular. He had a certain softness about him, both in manner and appearance. His sallow softness indicated a life of working indoors and at night. Trevor spoke to him as I walked to the front door.

'Hello; are you Mr von Einem?'

'Yes.'

'My name is Detective Kipling from the Major Crime Squad. I would like to ask you some questions about Mandrax.'

Von Einem's jaw set slightly.

'I don't want to answer any questions without my solicitor.'

'Who is your solicitor?'

'Helena Jasinski.'

Why didn't he want to speak to Trevor? I thought to myself. *This is a good sign. What has he got to hide?*

Obviously, people have a right to remain silent but suspicious police officers think that people who aren't frank and open have something to conceal.

Trevor could have continued and even entered von Einem's home with the search warrants that we both carried at the time. South Australia is unique in the allocation of general search warrants to detectives. Detectives, police bosses and sergeants in country police stations are issued with a permanent search warrant, which allows those officers to enter houses and to search for the evidence of a crime.

Trevor could have entered the house on production of his search warrant but we needed a reasonable suspicion that von Einem had committed a crime. We were getting close to having a reasonable suspicion but we weren't there yet. The courts could have easily thrown out any evidence we might have found if we didn't let him have a solicitor present. Trevor weighed up his options. Evidence thrown out versus von Einem having the opportunity to get rid of anything that might incriminate him — this was the dilemma which crossed our minds. Trevor wasn't prepared to stretch the legal boundaries that controlled investigations.

While this was happening we became aware of another person in the house. A small person was hovering around in the background — a woman. We saw an elderly lady standing in the passageway slightly behind von Einem, whose body dwarfed her. We soon learned that the woman was von Einem's mother and that she lived with her son.

Well, if this man was involved in any of the murders, they didn't happen here — not with his mother living with him, I reflected.

My thoughts were interrupted.

'Can you ring your solicitor?' Trevor asked impassively.

Von Einem then went back inside and rang Helena Jasinski. We did not know her background as a solicitor and we wondered how she would approach things. We overheard some of the conversation. She reinforced to von Einem that he should not say anything. He hadn't and now we didn't expect him to; however, he did agree to drive to the Angas Street police building in his own car and meet Helena there to give a statement. This gave us an opportunity to get some information about him and perhaps get a story from him about his movements when the boys went missing.

We drove to the Adelaide Police Station and von Einem followed us in his silver Toyota Corona hatchback. I was driving and made sure that we went slowly enough to ensure he stayed with us. I didn't want him turning off or getting separated from us at traffic lights. At the Angas Street building we even guided him into one of the police car parks to make sure he had a spot to leave his car. The three of us walked to the interview rooms of the Adelaide Police Station, which were wooden-lined cubicles immediately to the left of the front doors of the police building. We waited for Helena Jasinski to arrive and speak to her client.

A tall woman walked through the front doors of the police building. Her high cheekbones accentuated her attractiveness. We watched her walk to the counter, where she spoke to the staff on duty.

‘Hello, I’m Helena Jasinski. Can I speak to Detective Kipling, please?’

We overheard the conversation and Trevor moved towards her and spoke.

He explained to her the reason for our visit to von Einem’s home. He was up front about it. He wanted to speak to him about the murdered boys.

Von Einem was spoken to for a couple of hours. He confirmed he was a homosexual but denied any knowledge of the boys. Von Einem said that he was home in bed on Sunday, 5 June 1983, when Richard Kelvin was abducted. He said that he had the ’flu and he was in bed and off work for a week.

My first reaction was: *Well, if you were off work for a week, then you had the opportunity to be with Richard Kelvin.*

During Trevor’s interview, von Einem said that he suffered from a nervous condition and this led to questions about drugs in his possession.

‘What medication had you been prescribed for this nervous complaint?’ Trevor asked. He typed the response on the A4 piece of paper sitting in the Remington typewriter.

‘Serepax, Sinequan.’

‘You would have those medications in your house now?’

‘Yes.’

‘Would there be any other form of drug there?’

‘Rohypnol, which I need to sleep.’

Trevor asked him questions about the length of time he had lived in his house at Paradise and the length of time he had lived in his unit at Campbelltown before returning to questions about drugs.

'Have you ever been prescribed Mandrax tablets?'

'Yes, I have.'

'Would you tell me in detail about that, please?'

'I took Mandrax some five years ago for sleeping and wanted to get off them but I still have a sleep problem and my doctor put me on Rohypnol.'

'When was the last time you got Mandrax tablets?'

'It would have been about twelve months ago.'

More questions were asked about other matters before Trevor came back to the Mandrax. When detectives move the questions around, it sometimes puts the person being interviewed off guard. Von Einem may have thought Trevor had finished with that topic and started to relax, but Trevor again asked about the Mandrax.

'Do you have any left?'

'I have some left but I don't take them.'

'Where are they now?'

'They are at home.'

Trevor continued the interview and towards the end he asked:

'Did you kill Richard Kelvin?' No point beating around the bush. You never know what people will say.

'No.'

'Do you know who killed him?'

'No.'

'Do you know who abducted him?'

'No.'

'Could you conceivably abduct a youth, drug him, abuse him and then kill him?'

'No.'

'Why not?'

'I think it would be unethical of me; I shy away from violence of any description.'

They were interesting words. I didn't know what to make of them. They weren't words a normal person would use.

'Did you kill Alan Barnes?'

'No.'

'Do you know who did?'

'No.'

'Did you kill Neil Muir?'

'No.'

'Do you know who did?'

'No.'

'Did you kill Peter Stogneff?'

'No.'

'Do you know who did?'

'No.'

'Did you kill Mark Langley?'

'No.'

'Do you know who did?'

'No.'

Trevor asked him if he had any objection to the police examining his house and the police doctor taking a sample of his blood and hair. He allowed these things to happen. One of the police doctors, Noel McCleave, came to the Angas Street building and took a small sample of von Einem's hair, scraped under his fingernails and took a sample of his blood. These were standard samples taken by police when examining rape suspects. The blood allows tests to check whether or not it matches any sperm from a rape victim. The scraping from under the fingernails sometimes reveals tiny amounts of skin that have been scratched from a victim and, sometimes, pubic hair is left behind. These samples weren't expected to produce any evidence because sperm wasn't found on or in the boys and their skin wasn't scratched but we were working on the belief that the killers received sexual satisfaction from their crimes and these were standard tests.

We returned to von Einem's Paradise home the same day. Von Einem agreed that we could search his house. He returned to his home with Trevor and me. He agreed to leave his car with us to allow us to check its contents.

He didn't appear too worried about our interest in him. He was going to let us search his home. He is letting us keep his car for a couple of days. He could have refused, and lawyers could have disputed our legal right to search if we went ahead. He lives at home with his mother. All of these things suggested he had nothing to hide. But we couldn't ignore the possibility that he was involved. Some of his answers sounded funny. Especially saying it was unethical for him to kill someone.

Trevor Kipling led the return visit to Bevan von Einem's home. This time we had Des Phillips, one of our crime examiners, with us, along with Daryl Kruse from police photographics and Arch Kempster from our Fingerprint Section. We arrived at 4.15 p.m., eight hours after we had gone there in the morning.

Des put on his overalls and surgical gloves and entered the home, followed by Arch and Daryl. The lounge room opened up immediately you entered the front door. The only notable thing about the lounge was that it was ordinary, with a three-piece lounge setting, table, television and a few ornaments. The furniture was not cheap and nasty, but Christies wouldn't be auctioning any of it as antiques. Opposite the front door a narrow passage ran to the left from the lounge to the bedrooms, laundry and toilet. The carpets in the house were low quality. The passage carpet was a mild blue colour with a soft purple swirl in it. The kitchen was immediately behind the lounge. Trevor spoke to von Einem in the lounge while I did a preliminary search of his bedroom, which was at the front of the house nearest to the front door.

I walked on the dark blue bedroom carpet, which contrasted with the bright yellow bedspread covering his single bed. The bedspread had an orange check pattern over the base yellow colour. The bedspread was the brightest thing in the house. A white rectangular cupboard was standing against the wall alongside the bed. It was a standard affair with two doors either side of a central mirror which had drawers underneath it. A similar cupboard built without a mirror stood against the opposite wall. Small sideboards stood either side of the bedhead and at the foot of the bed on one side was an expensive looking harp. The harp was probably the most exceptional single item in the house. Police don't often see harps in the types of home they visit.

The first quick search found his carry bag alongside his bedhead. A credit card with von Einem's name on it helped prove the contents of the bag were his. I found a drug bottle in the bag. The bottle contained assorted drugs and a small slip of paper. On the paper were written the words 'Uncle

Bevan'. The bottle contained Sinequan, Serepax, Rohypnol and Valium.

The drug bottle in his bag did not contain Mandrax. I found three Mandrax drug bottles on the shelf of the cupboard with the mirror, but they were empty. They weren't in the carry bag or the bottle of assorted drugs. They could be anywhere, even buried in the yard, or hidden in the garage or the roof of the house. How do you find some pills if someone wants to hide them?

I used the element of surprise. Sometimes a direct question can catch people off guard, and this time it came as a surprise to von Einem. He was not expecting it.

I walked from the bedroom to the passageway where Trevor was standing with von Einem and his solicitor.

'Can you show us where the Mandrax are?'

'Behind the mirror — there is a ledge there.'

Von Einem walked into his bedroom and moved toward the white cupboard with the mirror in it. He reached into the left-hand side of the cupboard and pulled out two bottles of Mandrax from a ledge behind the mirror and gave them to me.

'There are tablets and capsules,' he said.

Bingo, I thought. Trevor and I had another win.

'How many would there be?' I said.

'There would be about forty capsules and ...' He hesitated and I asked:

'Is there anything else hidden in the room?'

'No.'

To this day I don't know why I did it but I looked inside the cupboard behind the mirror to see where von Einem had the drugs hidden. I saw a wooden ledge, which formed part of the framework of the cupboard that supported the mirror. Sitting on the ledge was another drug bottle. I reached in and took the bottle from the ledge. I read the word 'NOCTEC' on it. Before I said anything von Einem said, 'I don't use them much.'

'When I asked if you had anything else hidden in the room you said you didn't. That is right isn't it?'

'No, it isn't but I had mentioned to Helena about it in Angas Street.'

Now things were starting to look promising. Von Einem had Mandrax that was found in Mark Langley and Richard Kelvin and now we had found Noctec, which was also in Richard Kelvin. And the drugs were hidden.

Why would he want to hide these two drugs if he has nothing to hide? His other drugs weren't hidden.

Arch Kempster took photographs of the house inside and out. Other than the drugs, we didn't find anything of interest. Des Phillips took fibre samples from the house to check for one-way transfers — the movement of fibres from items in the house that might have got onto Richard Kelvin's clothes. He obtained fibre samples from the carpets in the house and the bedspread in von Einem's bedroom. He did not check for possible fibres from Richard Kelvin's clothing being in the house. Kelvin was wearing jeans and a blue T-shirt and they were made of common materials and colours that did not stand out. Daryl Kruse made a general check for fingerprints in von Einem's bedroom but did not find anything. However, what he did notice was that the door to the bedroom had been wiped clean. The fingerprint powder showed the marks left by the swirling motion of a cleaning cloth. Obviously, houses get cleaned and nothing could be made of this but Daryl was a very experienced fingerprint man and he was surprised just how much cleaning had been done in this bedroom.

We returned to the office about ten that night and gave work away. I was pretty tired after a long day and headed home. I didn't go to the Police Club, a square 1960s building that was built behind the Angas Street police building that we often visited at the end of a shift. On my way home I was thinking about things and, on a hunch, I decided to drive past von Einem's home. As I drove past, I saw a vehicle parked in the driveway. It wasn't von Einem's silver Toyota Corona hatchback or his older Ford Falcon.

Well, isn't that interesting? I thought.

I drove past and turned around. I stopped in the street and turned my lights off about five houses away. Parked in von Einem's driveway was a car, which would soon become very familiar to me. When I checked the registration details the next day, I learnt it belonged to an associate of von Einem. He may have been consoling von Einem after our visit to the house during the day. However, my suspicious mind suggested more sinister reasons. They would be talking about our visit. Talking about the implications of the seizure of the drugs.

Bevan Spencer von Einem just might be starting to get worried, I mused as I sat in my car parked in the darkened street, watching the house. The lounge room light was on. I gave it away at 1.30 in the morning. His friend was still there and I was satisfied that a close association had been confirmed.

Chapter 8

The Raids

The next morning we were back in the office. We didn't have enough evidence to arrest von Einem for any of the murders but he had to be a hot suspect. He was a homosexual who visited the beats. He had the reputation for picking up boys and sexually abusing them. He had the drug, Noctec, which was found in Alan Barnes and Mark Langley. He had three of the four drugs that were found in Richard Kelvin and two of the drugs, Mandrax and Noctec, were found hidden in his bedroom.

By this time Trevor Kipling was making all the running with the murder investigations. His leadership came naturally and was starting to show through. Glen Lawrie was smart enough to let this happen. Technically, Glen was the administration sergeant coordinating the investigation but he was also responsible for doing the same with another murder at the time, that of Louise Bell. Trevor had a determination about him that drove the investigation forward.

We needed to keep the pressure on our number one suspect so we drove to von Einem's workplace at South Road, Regency Park. It was critical that we got more evidence, so we quickly continued our search. With all murder investigations, the longer the investigation lasts, the less likely it is that the crime will be solved through the finding of evidence. Eight weeks had passed since Richard Kelvin had been abducted and we didn't want to lose any more time. Murders that have been committed a long time ago are more likely to be solved if the body of a missing person is found, the killer brags about what he has done, or a guilty conscience causes the killer to tell someone what they did. James Miller, who was involved with Christopher Worrell in committing the Truro murders, was distraught when Worrell was killed in a car crash. During this period of anguish he told a friend what Christopher Worrell was really like. And so he 'confessed' and talked about the murdered girls.

Von Einem worked in a new industrial area not far from the Regency Park TAFE College. The business where he worked was described by its name, Pipeline Supplies of Australia. As we pulled into the car park out the front, we commented that its location was just two kilometres away from where Alan Barnes was picked up on Grand Junction Road all those years ago.

Von Einem was the accountant at the firm. He started there in 1965 as a book-keeper who picked up accountancy skills as he went along. As such, he had a position of responsibility in the business where he worked. This power allowed him access to the building on weekends. The buildings sprawled out over the large block of land, which measured about 120 metres by seventy-five metres. A wide driveway on the left-hand side of the land allowed access to the warehouse, which was attached to the office building and ran for 100 metres down the block. The warehouse was accessed on that side by two large rollerdoors — big enough to take a truck. There was one in the centre of the warehouse and one right down the back. The high metal warehouse was about thirty metres wide.

On the right-hand side the ground was covered by bitumen and different areas held piles of pipes. The rectangular office building crossed the block and was shielded from the road by native trees.

We parked and moved to the reception area.

'My name is Detective Kipling from the Major Crime Squad. Can we speak to the manager, please?'

We spoke to Merv Martin and provided him with the general idea that our enquiries were about the murders and asked to see von Einem's office. Von Einem was not there. We were taken to a typical, unexceptional office of the day, about three metres by four metres with the walls painted in a light yellow or cream colour. It contained a desk, chairs, computer and filing cabinets. The search of von Einem's office gave us no further clues as to his night-time activities.

We again spoke with the manager and asked to be shown around his business, which he did without hesitation. We made a cursory search of the building and grounds, looking for a location where boys could be held captive or cut up. The business premise was not suitable for that sort of work and we found no evidence to show that Richard Kelvin had ever been on the premises. The warehouse was big and open and used for the storage of more pipes. The other areas of the office building included open space work areas, storerooms, meal rooms and toilets. There weren't any rooms or areas to keep anyone captive in nor were there any areas to cut up bodies without leaving a mess.

While we were checking von Einem's work, Ivan Sarvas and Des Phillips were minutely checking the maroon interior of the modern Toyota Corona hatchback owned by him and left at Angas Street. They put the car undercover in the workshops of the radio technicians and pulled the interior and boot apart looking for any evidence to suggest that Richard had been in the car.

We chased up the investigation that provided the first bit of evidence that started to give the investigation direction. Legendary police officer Sam Bass, a wrestler and motorcycle racer who later become a politician, had been working at the Holden Hill C.I.B. He investigated the case involving a boy who had been drugged with Mandrax before Richard Kelvin. We looked at this investigation to see what had happened with it.

The boy's name was George. He was a sixteen-year-old who was hitchhiking home about midnight on Saturday, 13 September 1982, six months after Mark Langley went missing and nine months before Richard Kelvin was abducted.

George was walking past an old ice works on Lower Portrush Road, which crosses the River Torrens at Royston Park in the eastern suburbs of Adelaide. A man in a bronze Ford Falcon was filling up his esky at the ice works and offered George a ride. The bespectacled man talked to him for a while as they were driving along and offered to take him to a party. There would be girls and booze there. George would have a good time.

The boy was taken to a house where some women lived. He had sex with one of them but then passed out. He arrived home in a taxi twenty-seven hours later with a one-half centimetre tear in his anus. George believed he had been drugged and abused, and reported it to the Holden Hill police.

Sam Bass found the taxi driver who took George home. He learned from the people in the house where George was taken that the man who picked him up was Bevan von Einem. Sam went to von Einem's work and spoke to him. Von Einem did not want to be spoken to at work and he agreed to meet Sam back at the Holden Hill Police Station where the short but muscular detective interviewed him.

Von Einem admitted picking up the boy, but said that George asked him for a lift. Von Einem agreed that he offered to take the boy to a party where there were drugs, booze and women. George was a willing party-goer, von Einem said. They drove to Alberton but the girls were not there. The homosexual who was at the house said they were working.

'When did the girls actually arrive home, then?' Sam Bass asked.

'About an hour after we got there; it must have been around 1.00 or 1.30 a.m.' von Einem answered. Sam methodically typed his replies onto a foolscap piece of paper.

'What did you do while waiting for the girls to come home?'

'We played music and had a drink. In fact, George drank a fair bit. He was drinking beer and brandy.'

'Who are the girls that live in the house and returned after you arrived?'

' "P" and "K".'

'What are their last names?'

'I don't know; they're just friends.'

He didn't know their last names but he could take a boy to their homes after midnight. What a lot of bullshit, I thought when I read what he said.

'What happened after the girls arrived at the house?'

'We were all drinking and playing music and sitting around talking.'

'During the evening, or at anytime while George was in your company, did you give him any type of tablet?'

'No. No.'

'Did you take any sort of tablet?'

'Yes.'

'What sort of tablets do you take?'

'Rohypnol, Serepax and Sinequan.'

'Where do you get these drugs from?'

'They are prescribed to me by my doctor.'

'What are they for?'

'Rohypnol is for sleeping. Serepax is to calm me down and Sinequan is an anti-depressant.'

'Why do you need all these tablets?'

'I have some personal problems and they help me. I have taken them for a long time.'

'Did you at any time give any of these tablets to the boy?'

'No.'

'What happened in relation to the boy while you were in the house?'

'He went into the bedroom with P and I think he had sex with her.'

'Did you go into the bedroom with P and the boy?'

'No.'

'How long did George and P remain in the bedroom?'

'I can't remember.'

'What happened after this?'

'P came out of the bedroom and we went on drinking.'

'The boy has admitted he had sex with P but states you were in the bedroom with them when the act started. What have you to say about this?'

'This is not right.'

'Did you go into the bedroom at all with George?'

'Yes.'

'Which bedroom did you go into?'

'P's bedroom at the front of the house.'

'What were the circumstances that caused you to go into the bedroom with George?'

'P went to sleep on the lounge where we were all talking and drinking and the others went to their rooms, so I went and slept on her bed.'

When I read the transcript of the interview, my immediate question was 'Why would P want to sleep on the lounge and not go back to bed with George?' She slept on the lounge because she knew that von Einem wanted a go at him.

'Did the boy come out of the bedroom with P?'

'No. He was pretty drunk and had gone to sleep or passed out.'

'How do you know this?'

'P said he had gone to sleep or something like that, when she came out of the bedroom.'

'After P went to sleep on the lounge then you went into her bedroom. Is that correct?'

'Yes.'

'What time was it that you went into the bedroom?'

'I have no idea. We were talking and drinking for a long time.'

'When you went into the bedroom, what happened?'

'I got on top of the bed and went to sleep.'

'Where was the boy?'

'In the bed, asleep.'

'During that night, did you sexually interfere with the boy?'

'No. I never touched him.'

'Did you actually get into the bed with him?'

'No, I slept on top of the bed all night and when I woke up he was still asleep and under the blankets. I was still lying on top of the bed.'

'I have had the boy medically examined and there is a scratch on the boy's anus. Have you any idea how it got there?'

'No, unless it happened when P had sex with him.'

'What time did you wake up?'

'I have no idea. It was late in the day.'

'Where was the boy when you woke up?'

'On the bed, asleep.'

'What did you do?'

'I got up and went out into the lounge. I think I had a shower and talked to the others.'

'When you say it was late in the day, what time roughly was it?'

'Late afternoon; I must have slept most of the day.'

'What happened to the boy?'

'He must have slept all day too and some of the night, as it was dark when he got up.'

'Why would a person sleep so long?'

'We drank over three-quarters of a bottle of brandy and was also drinking beer, and I think he was very drunk.'

Yes, I thought, but it was more than beer and brandy. He was popped some pills — Mandrax. The same drug that was given to Mark Langley and Richard Kelvin.

'What happened when he got up?'

'He had a shower and got dressed.'

'Did he do that on his own?'

'No, he was still pretty drunk and we helped him shower and get dressed. He said that he was still sleepy and he laid on the lounge.'

'How did the boy eventually get home?'

'He was placed in a taxi and sent home.'

'Who paid for the taxi?'

'I did.'

'How much did the taxi cost?'

'$15.'

'There was a piece of paper with the boy's address written on it. Who wrote this?'

'I don't know. I gave it to the taxi driver.'

'How old do you think the boy, George, is?'

'Seventeen or eighteen years old.'

'Did the boy go with you willingly at all times?'

'Yes.'

'Was the boy held forcibly at the house at Alberton at anytime?'

'Definitely not. He got drunk and fell asleep.'

'The boy has alleged in a statement to the police that you gave him two tablets that he believed from what you told him were No Doze tablets. Did you give him any sort of tablet?'

'No, I did not.'

If this was correct, why was he out to it for so long? I asked myself. At least we had another clue as to how these men got others to take drugs — telling the boys they were No Doze tablets.

'Why would the boy say this if it did not happen?'

'Probably to explain why he had been away so long. I don't really know. I did not give him any tablet or anything. He just drank a lot of alcohol.'

Von Einem was staying very cool-headed in the interview — just as he was with Trevor and me when we interviewed him. This was not a bad answer. This guy has an answer for everything.

'Is there anything else you wish to say about what happened with the boy?'

'No. I have nothing to hide.'

'I will be making further enquiries in relation to the incident involving the boy and I may well want to speak to you again about it. Do you understand?' said the detective.

'Yes.'

We got a team together and visited the house that George was taken to by von Einem. Here was a boy who was picked up by von Einem and later found to have Mandrax in his system. George was still adamant that when he had sex with one of the women von Einem was in the room when it happened. We needed to speak to the people who were living there. Obviously, they knew our main suspect.

The house was at Alberton. It had a low front wall. There was a path leading from the small gate to the home. The iron roof had been replaced with another one, which was shaped to look like roof tiles. The front door was in the centre of the house and there were two large windows on either side of it, which let light into the front bedrooms. An oil fire now filled the fireplace. The third bedroom ran down the side of the house, the kitchen sat at the rear and the toilet and the laundry filled up the rear of the house. The Hills Hoist sat in the centre of the rear lawn. The house belonged to the same era as von Einem's home; it wasn't as bland but it was more run down.

We didn't kick the doors down; the visit was low key and we made a cursory search of the house and yard. Different detectives were given the job of speaking to the three occupants. The most interesting thing we learned from the visit was about the three people who lived there. Two were transsexuals: persons who had changed from being men to women and the third was a man who was a homosexual.

P, the one George had sex with, was a transsexual. People might wonder how someone can have sex with a transsexual. It might seem weird, but P wasn't ugly and most couldn't tell the difference.

P, the transsexual, was taken to the Port Adelaide Police Station where I interviewed her about the drugging of George. I arrested her and she was charged with raping the boy. The arrest occurred because I believed she committed a crime but the arrest also was designed to put pressure on von Einem's friends, to encourage them to talk to us about him. P's arrest and charge got a little bit of attention in the media. 'Woman rapes boy' was the headline to the story and there were a few comments from men in the community.

'I wouldn't mind being raped by a woman,' was the general tone of what some said, but they didn't know the full story.

The others were interviewed about their knowledge of von Einem and our knowledge of the man increased a bit more. Our crime scene examiners took photographs and samples of fibres around the house but Des Phillips' first impressions didn't raise our expectation that we would find anything interesting. Also, the case against P was dismissed in the Port Adelaide Court when no evidence was put forward. There were difficulties proving that P had knowledge of the drugging and that she actually forced herself on George.

Trevor and I did one more raid shortly after the drugs were found in the boys. We visited the house of an Adelaide businessman, an associate of von Einem, and the man who owned the car that was parked in the driveway of von

Einem's home the night of our first visit. He lived in one of Adelaide's 'money' suburbs. The businessman already had been named as someone who should be spoken to about the missing boys. He had been mentioned in one of the hundreds of phone calls we received at Major Crime but we did not know he was an associate of von Einem. However, when Trevor interviewed von Einem, he said that he knew the businessman and when I saw the vehicle parked in the driveway of von Einem's home that night, this confirmed the relationship between the two men.

Trevor led the raid of the businessman's house and shop on 19 September 1983. The team was assembled and the group knew the routine. Trevor and I would go to the house and introduce ourselves while secondary team detectives, crime scene examiners, fingerprint experts and photographers would be parked around the corner waiting for the radio to call them to the house. If no-one was home, we would wait for the suspect to come home or we'd leave and come back another time when we thought the occupant would be there. We wouldn't go in without the occupant being present, otherwise the courts would criticise our actions and could discount any evidence that we might find.

The businessman was home, but he told us very little. He wouldn't give a statement but said he was a homosexual and had been a friend of von Einem for years. He denied any knowledge of the murders.

Immediately after searching the businessman's home we went to his shop, a two-storey building on one of Adelaide's main shopping roads. He had a young man working for him in his shop, also a homosexual. The business operated on the ground floor and administration was carried out upstairs. One of the rear second-floor rooms, however, was not used for administration. In it, a bare mattress was laid on the floor; nothing else was in the room.

That mattress would be able to tell some stories, I thought. Why would he have a mattress in a room of his business premises?

We seized the mattress but there was nothing on it to provide us with any evidence that was going to solve any of our murder investigations.

The businessman's cars were checked and samples of fibres were taken from the seats, boots and blankets in the cars. Police surveillance was placed on the businessman and he was followed over a lengthy period of time. His behaviour was almost compulsive/obsessive in the way that he would seek out male company. He would open up his business at the same time in the morning and close it punctually for lunch at twelve o'clock for an hour. He would drive his car to Number One beat and see what was happening there before checking out the other beats. At the end of his lunch break he would return to work. Although he lived very close to his business premises, the procedure would be repeated at the end of the day after he closed. He searched daily for young men to pick up.

Whenever he went out to a function at night, the businessman would go home via the beats. I was talking to one of the surveillance officers and he described how he was following our man in the city. This time he was walking along King William Street in the middle of the business district and a young boy was selling papers on the corner of King William and Grenfell Streets. The pedestrian lights turned red and the businessman stopped on the footpath back from the lights so he could 'perv' on the boy. When the lights did change for pedestrians to cross the road, the businessman remained where he was. He did not cross the road but remained where he was, perving on the boy. He missed a full cycle of lights before he moved on.

A young homosexual male was another associate of von Einem. He was young and, like most young boys, he was experimenting with life. He was trying out drugs and sex but the sex involved other men. He was of medium height and reasonably good looking. His youth did not prevent him from understanding the sexual desires of men and he accommodated their needs — for money.

This young man met von Einem on the banks of the Torrens at Number One beat on a weekend and, soon after, he moved into a unit at Collinswood, less than four kilometres from North Adelaide and the River Torrens. The unit was one of a number of modern apartment blocks that were being built in the area.

A phonecaller had suggested we should pay the young man a visit. Detectives Peter Woite and David Hunt visited the unit. The flat was the largest unit in a small block of flats. They did not raid the place — we need more information than an anonymous telephone call to kick down a door. There needs to be more evidence than that, such as a person having a criminal record for child abduction.

I interviewed the young man for four hours at the Angas Street police building. He said he was a homosexual but denied being a prostitute, although he did agree that some men gave him money but he said that the money was gifts and not given for sexual favours. He, too, denied knowing anything about the murders. Unfortunately, the visit to his unit and the interview revealed nothing new.

The initial raids were finished. It was time to regroup and consider what we had and what was to be the next move. Des and Ivan, the crime scene examiners, had to sort out the physical evidence, the samples of fibres and material that had been collected from the various locations. The teams of detectives still had a lot of inquiries to make, many relating to von Einem but most dealing with other leads. We were still trying to find evidence of snuff movies, and other names were being followed as potential sources who might know about the murders. Also, there were some interesting observations being made by Des and Ivan. They were showing just how much murder investigation is a team effort.

Von Einem denied knowing or having anything to do with Richard Kelvin when he was first interviewed on 28 July 1983. However, with many police investigations, once the right suspect is found, the case gets stronger and stronger. We now had evidence that von Einem was picking up and drugging young boys but that didn't mean that he killed boys.

As the weeks and months passed following the visit to von Einem's home Des Phillips had dried the clothing of

Richard Kelvin and searched for trace elements. He handed over tiny fragments of paint, small pieces of coloured fibre and hair to the forensic scientists. Des, Ivan and the forensic scientists were very cautious. The Splatt Royal Commission, which recently challenged the evidence provided by police and forensic scientists, was still very fresh in their minds. However, Des did indicate that the fibres on Richard's clothing were similar in appearance to fibres from von Einem's home but he wasn't the expert. Sandra Young from the Forensic Science Lab would have to check them.

There were also hairs which were found on Richard's clothing that were starting to look interesting. The majority of the hairs on Richard's clothing were his own but there were a few hairs that were different from Richard's and they looked very much like those hair samples that were taken from von Einem! If we could show the fibres and hair matched, then it would prove that our main suspect, Bevan Spencer von Einem, was with Richard Kelvin. We might just have a case.

Now it was time to visit a few of von Einem's other associates and other people who had been nominated as possible suspects. There was the lawyer, the doctor, the second person whom von Einem said was one of his best friends, another transvestite and a couple of others that needed to be visited just as we had done with von Einem. Five raids were planned to happen on the morning of 12 October 1983.

Trevor Kipling planned and organised the raids. Two detectives were given a nominated suspect to interview, and a crime scene examiner was allocated to go with the detectives. If there was more than one suspect at an address, then only one crime scene examiner went to the address. Resources were starting to be stretched thin by this time and we had to manage as best we could. Also, the raids were planned to occur at the same time to prevent different suspects ringing one another and warning each other what was happening.

On that day, Trevor and I returned to von Einem's home. After we arrived, von Einem phoned his lawyer, Helena Jasinski. Trevor explained the reason for our new visit to the house and she advised her client not to say anything. He wasn't talking anyway and we didn't expect him to. Helena Jasinski followed us into the house and was present as we seized the bedspread from von Einem's bed and pulled up the carpet from his bedroom floor. Helena and von Einem objected, claiming our actions were unusual, but we knew that it was going to be important, as fibres on Richard Kelvin's clothing were looking more and more certain to be from von Einem's bedroom. We didn't have to pull up carpet from the passageway and lounge as a carpet square made of the same material was laying in the passageway near the front door.

By this time, Lee Haddon had finished with the trial of Dr Millhouse and he was helping out with some of the administration work. Lee had an initial connection with our team, having asked Peter Woite on 2 August 1983 to try and locate the person who first mentioned von Einem's name as someone we should speak to about the murder of Alan Barnes. Obviously, that person knew von Einem and he probably knew things about him that we didn't. We could learn things from him, or at least discover that he had a grudge against von Einem and was just setting him up. It was important that we found out either way. Later this person became known as ‘B’. He told us things about von Einem that were so bizarre that they had to be true.

Chapter 9

The Associate

Peter Woite was given the task of finding B. He learned that he was interstate, living in Melbourne, so Peter travelled to Victoria to speak with him, but B had moved again just prior to his arrival. Now, he was believed to be living in Mildura on the Murray River. Peter contacted local detectives to see if they could find him but they didn't have any luck and the trail went cold after that. We chased up family members — coincidentally, his father lived in a suburb near von Einem, while his sister lived in the northern outskirts of Adelaide — neither of them knew of B's exact whereabouts. Peter kept running into a blank wall.

Revisiting the enquiry in October 1983, I drove to B's sister's house at Gawler, north of Adelaide, but she wasn't home, so I left a message for her to phone me. I spoke with her a couple of times on the telephone and she said that she would try and get him to ring me.

I was sitting in the offices of the Major Crime Squad when B telephoned in November 1983. B said that he would not come to the police building but would meet me at a hotel. We decided to meet that afternoon. I was sitting at a table in a city hotel when B walked in with another young man. B looked soft but not effeminate although his male friend looked gay. He was prissy and subservient to B. I bought both of them a drink and B told his friend to sit elsewhere. He immediately moved off without saying anything and sat at another table. I told B that I wanted to speak to him about von Einem. He started asking me questions, testing me, assessing whether or not I could be trusted. Then he told me a few things that whetted my interest. He said that he picked up boys with von Einem, drugged them and had sex with them.

I've got to get this guy on side. This guy's information is dynamite, I thought.

I asked him to come to the Angas Street police building so I could get a statement from him. He didn't want to come straight away because he had his friend with him. He said that he would come in the next day.

I was sitting at my desk in the Major Crime office when a constable at the front desk rang to tell me B was at the front counter. I went down and greeted him.

'Thanks for coming in,' I said.

'No worries.'

'Look, we'll go to an interview room upstairs where it is quieter.'

Top Left: Alan Barnes – the first young man to disappear. *Top Right:* Neil Muir – whose dismembered body was found in garbage bags in the Port River. *Above:* Peter Stogneff – the youngest of the five who disappeared. *Middle Right:* Mark Langley – who was last seen near the banks of the River Torrens. *Right:* Richard Kelvin – the last of the missing boys.

Opposite Page Top: Number 1 Beat – a meeting place for homosexuals on the banks of the River Torrens close to the centre of Adelaide. *Opposite Page Middle:* The country road near Middle Beach where the sawn-up remains of Peter Stogneff were found. *Opposite Page Bottom:* Crime scene examiners checking for clues after Peter Stogneff was found. *Top Left:* Police recover the remains of Neil Muir at Mutton Cove. *Top Right:* A replica of the zodiac medallion and silver chain missing from Mark Langley. *Above:* Police divers search the River Torrens before Mark Langley was found in the Adelaide Hills.

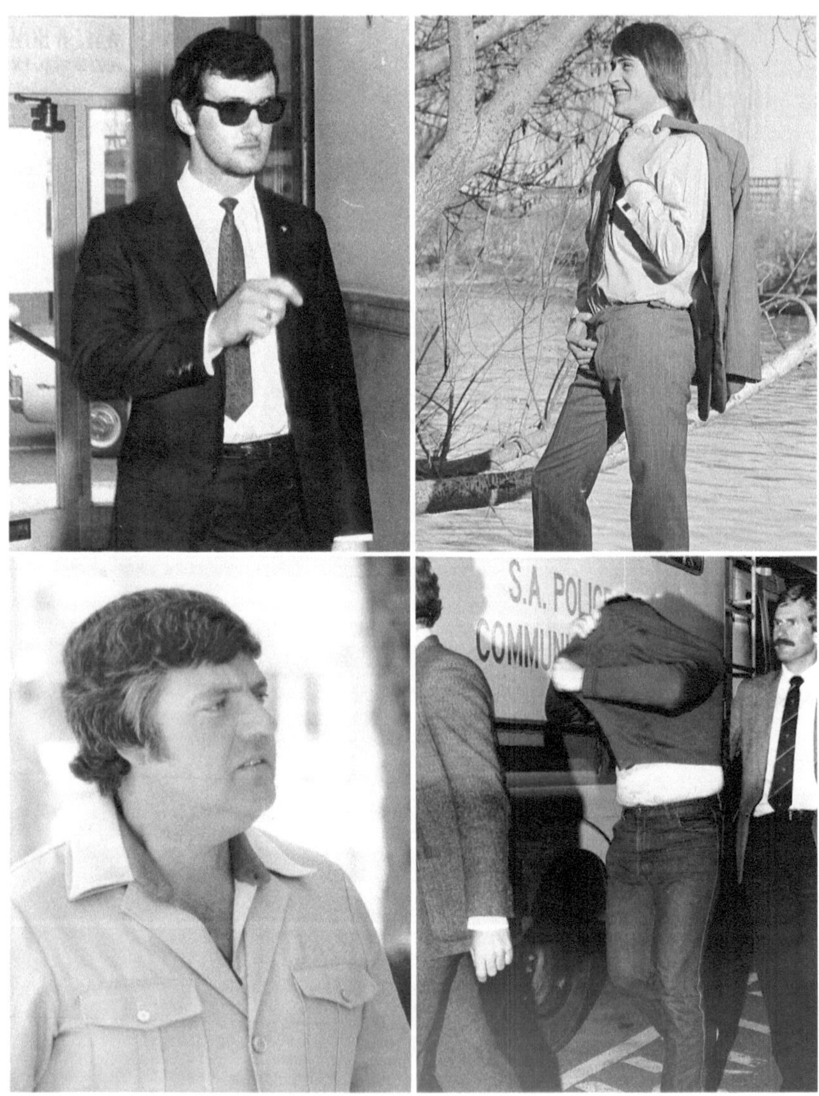

Top Left: Bevan Spencer von Einem at the coroner's inquest into the drowning of Professor Duncan at Number 1 Beat. *Top Right:* Roger James, who was also thrown into the River Torrens with Professor Duncan. Von Einem took him to hospital after James climbed from the river with a broken leg. *Above Left:* Detective Trevor Kipling, the lead detective in the investigation. *Above Right:* The author taking von Einem to be charged with the murder of Richard Kelvin. (Detective Mark Ryan partially obscured.) *Opposite Page Top:* O'Connell Street, North Adelaide, showing the bus stop in front of the delicatessen where Richard Kelvin was last seen. *Opposite Page Middle:* Ward Street, North Adelaide, where Richard Kelvin lived. He was 50 metres from home when he was abducted. *Opposite Page Bottom:* Police cadets searching the scrub for evidence after finding the body of Richard Kelvin.

Schweppes
RESTAURANT
TAXI

CAN YOU HELP?

WANTED

About 8 p.m. on Sunday, June 5, 1983, RICHARD DALLAS KELVIN disappeared in the North Adelaide area.

The police are anxious to locate a light-colored EJ Holden sedan which has been described as being in good condition. This vehicle is fitted with a tow bar and two mirrors, one on each front mudguard.

The occupants of this vehicle have used the names "Doug" and "Mark" and may be able to assist police with their enquiries into the possible abduction of Richard Kelvin.

REWARD

Notice is hereby given that a reward of up to FIVE THOUSAND DOLLARS ($5000) will be paid by the Government of South Australia to the person who first gives information which results in the finding of the missing person, RICHARD DALLAS KELVIN.

The allocation of the reward will be at the discretion of the Commissioner of Police.

The urgent assistance and cooperation of the public is especially sought in this matter. Any information, which will be treated as confidential, may be given at any time of the day or night at any Police Station or at Police Headquarters, telephone 218 [illegible].

This is the type of T-shirt Richard Kelvin was wearing when last seen. Anyone who remembers seeing a youth dressed in this style in the North Adelaide area at the time of Richard's disappearance is asked to contact police.

This is the most recent picture available of Richard Kelvin. He is described as being 180 centimetres (5 ft. 11 ins.) in height, with short fair hair and blue eyes. When he disappeared he was wearing blue jeans, white sneakers and a blue T-shirt identical to the one shown on this page.

NOTE: The car pictured resembles the car sought by police. The car police seek also has two mirrors, one on each front mudguard, and a tow bar.

This notice is inserted by SA Police and *The Advertiser*.

Please keep it in a prominent place. People such as shop owners are asked to further assist by displaying it prominently.

PLEASE DISPLAY THIS PAGE PROMINENTLY IF YOU CAN

Opposite Page Top Left: Rob and Richard Kelvin hamming it up at home. *Opposite Page Top Right:* The full page *Advertiser* broadsheet seeking help from the community. The car was a false lead. *Opposite Page Middle:* Von Einem's house in the Adelaide suburb called Paradise. *Opposite Page Bottom:* Airstrip Road, leading to the site where Richard Kelvin's body was found. He was held captive for five weeks. *Top Left:* Prosecutor (now Judge) Brian Martin. *Top Right:* Assistant prosecutor Paul Rofe. *Above Left:* Defence counsel (now Judge) Barry Jennings. *Above Right:* A later photograph of assistant defence counsel Helena Jasinski.

Top Left & Top Right: Von Einem at the time the jury visited various locations mentioned by Brian Martin during the trial. *Above Left:* Doctor Ross James, pathologist, who gave evidence in the trial. *Above Right:* Scientist Sandra Young, who gave important forensic evidence during the trial.

There were interview rooms downstairs at the Adelaide Police Station but I didn't want any distractions and I didn't want anyone who came into the police station seeing B talking to the police. He could be an important witness.

I took B to the first of two detective interview rooms on the second floor of the Angas Street building, past the reception desk for the Bureau of Criminal Intelligence. There are two interview rooms, including one with a two-way mirror. Detectives and bosses accessed the viewing area by going into an adjacent office and stepping into a small room, not much bigger than a broom closet, which did not let in light which could possibly destroy the effect of the two-way mirror. The mirror allowed private viewing of suspects sitting in the interview room. Obviously, a suspect could be watched to observe any mannerisms or if he was trying to hide any property or drugs in his clothes but I don't know of any cases where the private viewing produced any additional evidence.

I spoke to B for six hours and typed his statement. It was eighteen pages long with seven additional pages of notes and drawings. What he told me was sensational.

He was was in his early twenties and had been active in the gay scene for about five years. He said he was bisexual — he also had sex with women. He said that he was now heterosexual but the sweet young guy with him at the pub made this statement questionable. B had first met von Einem in June 1979. By my calculations, that would have made it just before Alan Barnes was murdered.

Their first encounter was on a Sunday afternoon at the Torrens, near a boathouse. B described Number One beat near Jolly's Boathouse on the south side of the river. He knew the area well. He mentioned the half-dozen boat sheds on the southern bank and the other three on the northern side near where Mark Langley disappeared. B said he was sitting on the lawns covering the banks of the river when von Einem approached him and asked if he wanted a drink. Their relationship developed from there. B knew von Einem was a homosexual but said he never had sex with him.

I recorded B's words. I typed them directly onto paper as he recounted his graphic story. Taped interviews, either by tape recorder or video recorder, weren't being done in 1983. We were still typing word by word. B described von Einem's activities and said that von Einem had his own beat. His beat was not one of those around Adelaide's public toilets, as have been described previously, he had his own beat on which he cruised to pick up boys. I kept typing as fast as I could to keep up with the story.

'King William Street between North Terrace and Scotty's Motel ... that was his beat. He used to cruise up and down from Parliament House through North Adelaide to Scotty's Motel and back again. He used to do it all the time.'

Scotty's Motel is just to the north of Adelaide, past the inner suburb of North Adelaide. It's well known to people because a tall statue of a Scotsman stands on the front wall of the motel. At the other end of von Einem's beat, South Australia's Parliament House stands on the corner of King William Street and North Terrace, next to Adelaide's Festival Theatre, which separates Parliament House from the River Torrens. On the opposite side of the road, about 100 metres away, is Number One beat. The main road out of town starts at Parliament House, crosses the River Torrens, goes through North Adelaide via O'Connell Street, where Richard Kelvin saw Karl Brooks off at the bus-stop, and continues north past the motel.

B graphically described how, together, he and von Einem had picked up two boys.

'I don't know where I met up with Bevan that night but it was at night-time, probably a Saturday night; but it was definitely after midnight when we picked up two hitchhikers.'

I started to learn about von Einem's *modus operandae*. The duo picked up the boys in von Einem's bronze Falcon sedan and offered them a drink.

'We gave them booze and Bevan gave them heaps of Rohypnol and they went out to it in the car. He would give them at least eight to ten Rohypnol. Bevan always keeps booze in the car. Normally, there is an esky in the boot and one on the back seat, which he keeps covered with clothes in case he is pulled up by the cops.'

The mention of Rohypnol — possibly one of the drugs which were in Richard Kelvin's system — was a great piece of information, further completing the jigsaw. Speculation had always existed over the disappearance of Mark Langley. He was tall and strong. He worked as a plumber, which built up his muscles and strength. People wondered how someone could abduct a growing young man of his size. Mark Langley, as with all the boys, showed no signs of defence wounds, which are caused when a victim tries to protect himself, and are very obvious, say, in knife attacks. The victim will have cuts to his hands and forearms, caused when the hands are raised trying to fend off the attacker.

Cuts to the leg happen when the victim kicks out trying to hold off the attacker, and are less common, as are defence wounds when a shooting occurs. The speed of a bullet will not allow the victim to do much. However, if the victim sees what is about to happen, then the victim may raise his hands to cover his face in fear. If the gun is fired towards the victim's head, then the bullet may hit a hand or arm before passing through to the skull.

I imagined an angry and upset Mark Langley storming away from his friends parked on War Memorial Drive. He already had drink in him from the party. He was probably walking on King William Road or one of the nearby roads thinking about how he was going to get home when a good Samaritan stopped and asked if he wanted a lift. The driver would offer a few soothing words after he learned that Mark was upset and angry. The words would be followed by the offer of a drink from the driver, who looked harmless. The drink would help Mark calm his anger and settle him down. If 'rollies' were placed in the drink, then the combination of drugs and alcohol would soon put Mark Langley out to it. Then he was simply under the control of the driver, who could become the hidden Mr Hyde, our sexual sadist. We couldn't prove this scenario but it was a distinct possibility. If von Einem didn't do it, then someone like him did — perhaps even a mate of his did it.

Perhaps even this person did it, I was thinking as I typed B's words on the blank pieces of paper rolled into the typewriter.

✪ ✪ ✪

Von Einem's partner continued to tell me his story.

'After about ten minutes they were complaining that they were too pissed to drink and Bevan said, "Take the Rohypnol" and that would sober the kids up. That is what he said to them to get them to take the tablets. They were small white or yellow tablets about the same size as diazepam. Diazepam is Valium. I know that they were Rohypnol because I asked him what they were and he said "rollies" and I saw the word "Rohypnol" on the bottle.'

In the years that B knew von Einem, our main suspect was living in a unit at Campbelltown, one neighbourhood away from von Einem's suburb of Paradise. Von Einem moved to Paradise in the early months of 1983. B described how they took boys back to the unit. They could do this, he said, because von Einem's mother was away every second weekend. She would go and visit a cousin, Beryl Alcorn, at Lower Hermitage, a country area just outside Adelaide's suburbs in a gully at the bottom of the Adelaide Hills.

B said the unit comprised two bedrooms, lounge, kitchen, bathroom and small laundry. It was one of three units built nearly at the end of a no-through road and the unit was the last in the block. They drove up the concrete driveway alongside the units and stopped outside the front door to carry the boys inside.

'We drove down the driveway and turned left and parked. The back door of the car ended up right next to the front door of the unit. It made it easy to carry the kids into the unit ... Bevan took the kid by the arms and I had the legs and we carried him into the bedroom, which was Bevan's, and we put him straight onto the bed with his head on the pillow ... We brought the second one in the same way and dropped him on the lounge room floor. I then went back into Bevan's bedroom because he asked me to get [the boy] undressed.'

B continued to tell his story to me. He knew a lot about a side of von Einem that was very sinister and sick.

'Before we undressed him [the one in von Einem's bedroom], he showed me his pill collection, which was on top of shelves on the opposite side to his single bed. He had Rohypnol, Mandrax, Valium, Palfium and I think that there were a couple of other jars there but I cannot remember just what they were.'

B's comments about the different type of drugs fitted with what we knew about von Einem. During the visit to his home on 28 July 1983, we found those assorted drugs in his carry bag and the Mandrax and Noctec hidden on the ledge behind the mirror of his cupboard in the bedroom. I was mentally comparing what B was telling me with what we knew to be true to check the truth of his story.

Von Einem used to live in a unit when Detective Rod Hunter spoke to him about Alan Barnes. That checks out.

'Kippers' and I better have a look at that address.

He did have a Falcon before getting his new car. That checks out.

The drugs check out.

B continued to describe what they did to the two drugged hitchhikers in von Einem's unit.

'We took one shoe and sock off each, were both helping each other, and left his shirt. He was lying on top of the bed, and we both went out and undressed the other one in the lounge room. Bevan then went into his bedroom and closed the door.'

I thought that it was interesting that the two of them undressed each boy. They didn't undress them separately. If von Einem was involved in the murders, he was big enough to carry the boys by himself but here he was working with another person to undress someone. Here he was picking up boys, drugging them and then undressing them with help from another person.

'I did not touch the one in the lounge room. I would have but he wasn't good looking and he was rolling around as though he was going to be sick.'

He wasn't good looking and was going to be sick! What a casual way to tell me what he did. B was talking to me in a very matter-of-fact way. There was no indication of guilt or remorse.

You haven't got a guilty conscience about any of this, I thought.

Then B's story became even more astonishing and grotesque.

'When I went in the young blond [guy] was still on the bed; he was facing the wall and his knees were drawn right up to his chest. Bevan was kneeling on the floor next to the bed. Bevan was holding a torch up the boy's arse and he pulled this rod out of his arse as I walked in the door. Bevan's light was off but I had the light on in the lounge and that threw light into the room. As I said, as I opened the door I saw Bevan pull this crochet needle-type thing out of his arse ... Anyway he pulled the rod out and then slowly pulled the torch out and I saw that it was on. When he pulled the rod out he put it down on the floor. He did the same with the torch after turning it off. I know that he was angry when I walked in.'

Incredible! Unbelievable! But I was certain it was true. B was too detailed with his descriptions to make this up. Besides, he knew about von Einem's unit, his car and he knew about the drugs. He even mentioned the names of the drugs that we were interested in. I interrupted B and gave him my pen and asked him to draw the shape of the rod and torch on one of the blank white pieces of typing paper. He did some sketching and continued telling his story.

'I told him that I wanted to go because the one that I was with was waking up, but it was just an excuse to get away. Bevan said that he would kill the cunt if he woke up. He asked for me to wait and help him get them dressed and take them to someone else's house. He said that they will sleep all day with the Rohypnol and that he wanted to get them to this drag queen's place where they could sleep it off.'

A drag queen — more information that fitted with what we already knew.

'We dressed both of them and carried them to the back seat of the car and propped them up each side of the back seat. Bevan said that if we are stopped by the cops to say that they are both drunk and that we are taking them home. Bevan drove and I was sitting in the front passenger's seat. I think that we must have taken back streets ... I remember what the house looked like ... three drag queens lived there; one was half-Maori and the other two were white. The name, P, rings a bell but I cannot be sure.'

Well, Miss P comes up again. George, the other hitchhiker, was taken to P's place when he was drugged.

B was taken home and he rang von Einem during the week at work to find out what happened to the boys.

'... he said they slept it off until midday the next day and they went home. The only other thing that I remember is that the one in the lounge was rolling his head and said a few things when we were getting him dressed. Bevan was a bit rough with him. Just throwing his legs around and things like that and he gave him another couple of rollies to keep him quiet. He gave him a bit of water from the kitchen to wash them down.'

During the hours that I typed his statement, B told me another story, describing exactly the same type of deviant behaviour. He described how he met von Einem near one of the boatsheds at Number One beat at about 7 p.m. on a Saturday two or three weeks after they picked up the first two boys. They cruised around in von Einem's car, scored a bit of grass and went to the Duke of York Hotel for a drink. Later in the evening they picked up two youths about eighteen years of age who were hitchhiking.

One had tattoos; B said that he saw them on his legs later on, when they were undressed at the flat of another associate of von Einem — not at von Einem's unit this time and at a different place from the other associate's.

B said that when they arrived, the drag queen was expecting them. They went to the flat, smoked a couple of bongs and von Einem offered the hitchhikers rollies after pretending to take a handful himself. The lads downed about eight or nine rollies each with some beer and, after a couple more drinks, they passed out.

One of the drugged hitchhikers had said he wanted to go to sleep and the drag queen helped him into her bedroom where von Einem helped the drag queen to undress him and put him into her double bed. At this stage, B said he left to go to Patches Disco, a gay club, on North Terrace in the city, while von Einem and the drag queen stayed with the hitchhikers. Later, B asked the drag queen what happened after he left. She said that the one with tattoos fucked her and they left next morning when they woke up. The drag queen said she didn't know what von Einem got up to with the other one.

B then described a third time, when they picked up another boy. It was the following Saturday night and again they met at Number One beat after B rang to see if they were going to get together. Obviously, B didn't distance himself from von Einem after the first time they picked up hitchhikers. It was just like Miller and Worrell with the Truro murders. Miller said that he didn't touch the girls. B is saying that he left before anything happened but here he was continuing to pick up boys and continuing to ask von Einem if they were meeting and going out.

B is a deviate just like von Einem.

This time they picked up a really young hitchhiker at about seven in the evening. B said that he was only thirteen or fourteen. Von Einem gave him cans of beer, and after a while von Einem asked if he wanted any pills, which the kid took. After about 20–30 minutes, the kid became drowsy and von Einem took him back to his unit. Von Einem's mother was away again. This time von Einem carried him inside the unit by himself. He picked him up by placing one arm under the armpit and the other arm under his legs. He carried him inside and put him on the bed. B said that he undressed him by himself. He described his feelings about the age of the boy.

'I got pissed off with Bevan ... I saw how really young this guy was ... I saw then that this boy had no pubic hair. His clothes were on the floor next to the bed but Bevan was still dressed. I saw the torch and rod on the end of the bed again.'

He was mucking around with kids — this guy was describing the actions of a person who has no morals and no concerns about his behaviour.

'I asked Bevan to take me back to town. He did so and I think that he dropped me off at the Mars Bar. The kid was left at the flat. He was left lying on the bed undressed. I said to him going to town about how young the kid was and he said that it didn't matter.'

'It didn't matter.' What a pair these two were, I thought.

B's comments not only clearly showed what he and von Einem got up to for entertainment, but he was also, during our lengthy conversation, mentioning quite a few other names. There was von Einem's mate, the businessman, who drove fancy cars. There were drag queens and transsexuals, who lived in different parts of town, and who were known by von Einem. It was obvious he had a wide circle of associates including gays, lesbians, drag queens and transsexuals.

But why did B continue to remain friendly with von Einem?

'I only used to hang around Bevan because he used to supply the grass and piss. Occasionally, he used to give me money — $40-$50. He gave me the money because I asked for it and he liked me. I was gay then but I had never had sex with Bevan.'

His comments were a revelation and confirmed other stories the police team heard over the months the investigation was going on. I pondered over his statement but after six hours I was exhausted — concentrating, conducting an interview for such a long time is mentally tiring work.

I met B again two days later and drove him around with Mark Ryan, another detective who was seconded to Major Crime. B pointed out various addresses to me — where he used to live, the beats, von Einem's house, his old unit, several drag queens' homes in the western suburbs and where different people von Einem knew lived.

Bevan von Einem, the plain, softly-spoken accountant, was the surprise in all of these unfolding discoveries. He appeared harmless. People thought that he was a nice guy or, even if they didn't really like him, they still thought he was soft. During our investigation we learned that von Einem would take his mother to Tupperware parties and, even then, he would not leave her at the party but stay with the other elderly women, sitting to one side waiting for his mother, ready to take her home after the party finished.

'What a lovely man,' the women would say. Some of them would wish that their sons were as considerate as Bevan, but these women had not the faintest idea of the 'other' von Einem.

These women did not speak to people who saw him one night laying back in the front seat of his car outside the

Mars Bar nightclub in Gouger Street, Adelaide. He called over people to show them the pencil he was sticking into his penis. We learned that von Einem was a mild-mannered 'Clark Kent'. He even looked a bit like a Clark Kent-type person, but he was not a good guy in civilian clothing. Bevan Spencer von Einem was a superdeviate. If von Einem was our serial killer, then his appearance and public persona would allow him to get away with those types of crimes.

We had meetings with the Department of Public Prosecution, including Brian Martin, the Director, and his assistant, Paul Rofe. Both men were ex-footballers. Brian Martin had played for the Sturt Football Club in the South Australian National Football League while Paul Rofe had played in the amateur league. Both were tall men, intelligent and astute.

Brian had been kept informed of the potential evidence as we were finding it and several meetings were held. Forensic scientists, Bob Lokan and Sandra Mattner, were there at the meeting on Thursday, 3 November 1983. Sandra, who later married and became Sandra Young, spoke about the fibre, hair and paint that had been seized at von Einem's home. She confirmed that the fibres found on Richard's clothing were starting to match fibres from the von Einem home. A lot of the discussion revolved around having suitable experts giving the evidence. Bob Lokan believed that it was necessary for overseas experts to come to South Australia to check their findings. Gerry Edwards, the Superintendent in charge of Major Crime, offered to submit a report to the police commissioner requesting extra funding from Treasury to get an overseas scientist to Australia.

The forensic scientists were being cautious. They wanted to be sure of their findings and wanted to do more work, but Trevor had read the statement of B the day after I typed it, and he wasn't going to wait any longer. He had had enough. He'd spoken to police psychologists during our investigations and they thought that our serial killers could strike again. At our meeting with the D.P.P. on Thursday, 3 November 1983 Trevor said he was going to make his move.

We drove to Paradise and parked a couple of houses away from von Einem's house as we did a little over three months previously. We walked to the front door just as we did in July. Again we walked on the lawn to the front door — old habits die hard. We weren't concerned about losing evidence this time. We had enough evidence. It was time to act. Trevor knocked on the front door.

No answer.

Here we were all prepared to arrest von Einem for murder after all of this time and he wasn't home! I went down the driveway to the side fence that joined the house to the garage. The side gate was locked. I jumped over to have a look around the back yard. I started to move to the rear door as I heard Trevor yell.

'Bob.'

I jumped the rear fence to see von Einem's Toyota stop in the driveway of his house. He parked as he normally did, in line with the front door. His mother sat in the front left-hand seat. Von Einem got out of the driver's seat and faced Trevor, who at first was about two metres away but then approached von Einem to be as close as a metre from him.

'Mr von Einem, as you know this is Detective O'Brien and my name is Kipling from the Major Crime Squad. I wish to inform you that I am arresting you and that you will be charged with the murder of Richard Kelvin. I must also inform you that you are not obliged to answer any further questions and whatever you do say may be used in evidence. Do you understand that?'

Von Einem remained standing by the car and was silent for a moment before replying with a couple of words.

'Yes, well.' He was searching for words. Von Einem always had a story. He always had an answer. This time he struggled for words.

'Oh, Bevan. What's going on?' Thora von Einem asked her son as she moved around from the passenger side of the vehicle towards the man who had just been arrested for murder. She was upset.

Von Einem stood there in his blue jeans, light-coloured shirt and brown jumper. He was not angry. He was not upset. He just stood there without displaying any emotion, probably just as he has failed to show any emotion for most of his adult life.

Trevor pointed towards the police car and the three of us moved towards it. Von Einem was placed in the rear of the police car, behind the front passenger's seat. Trevor moved around to the rear of the car, got in and sat next to him and I hopped into the driver's seat.

We drove in silence to the Angas Street police building. Behind the building was the old City Watch House. The watch house was a two-storey brick building with two wings — one for female prisoners and one for males. The female side was rarely occupied but the other side was always busy. Often the ground floor would fill and the spillover would have to be moved to the cells upstairs. Most of the cells accommodate one person but several had two slabs of wood fastened to the wall that served as a bed and allowed for two people in a cell. Each slab of wood had an extra piece of wood attached to one end. That was the pillow. Dark grey blankets were issued for warmth. It was one of the first places I worked after I graduated from the police academy.

The padded cells were around the back of the ground floor for prisoners who were violent or were trying to hurt themselves. The padding covers the four walls of the cell while the floor is covered by linoleum with a metal plug in the middle to allow vomit, faeces and urine to be washed away. Prisoners who go into the padded cells are stripped and left in darkness. The blackness tends to calm them. If they are trying to hurt themselves, the padding covered by heavy canvas prevents any injury even if they throw themselves against it or hit their heads against it — unlike metal bars, which can cause a bit of damage. Invariably, anyone visiting the cells to see what they were like was placed in a padded cell to get the real experience of it.

We pulled into the laneway next to the police building and moved towards the City Watch House. I walked alongside von Einem with Trevor walking a couple of paces in front, striding towards the cells of the City Watch House. Trevor checked through the window to see if the charge sergeant was free. He was and Trevor opened the door and walked von Einem to the window in front of the sergeant.

'What's the charge?'

'Murder,' Trevor said.

The Watch House sergeant looked up and stared at von Einem for a second and the cell guard standing nearby quietly signalled his mate to come from the fingerprint room. The sergeant looked down at his charge book.

'Name?'

'Bevan von Einem,' said the accountant.

'Do you have a middle name?'

'Spencer.'

'Address?'

Von Einem gave his address at Paradise.

'Arresting officers?'

'Kipling and O'Brien — Major Crime Squad,' Trevor said.

'Place your property on the counter,' the sergeant said to von Einem.

The prisoner emptied his pockets and placed their contents in front of the sergeant who was filling out the charge book. We searched von Einem, ensured that his pockets were empty, and counted his money in front of the sergeant. The cash and property were placed in a dirty white canvas bag with a number on it, which was then recorded in the charge book. Trevor opened von Einem's handkerchief, saw that it was empty and returned it to him before removing his belt and shoelaces. Too many prisoners have hanged themselves over the years with items as tiny as shoelaces. It was important we didn't lose this prisoner.

Chapter 10

The Case

We had learned a lot about von Einem from B. His statement clarified so many things that we could only suspect. By this time other boys had been found who von Einem had picked up and drugged but they couldn't say what happened once they were out to it. B completed the picture. We now could be confident that von Einem picked up boys and drugged them and abused them with different objects.

The picking up of the hitchhiker, George, and the taking of him to Alberton where the 'girls' were was just one example of his activities. On that occasion he openly offered tablets to the boy but said they were No Doze. Other times von Einem would quietly put drugs into alcohol without the drinker knowing. Alcohol loosened the inhibitions of the boys so they would be more open to taking drugs, and the booze also increased the potency of the drugs. Once the boys were slipped a few Mickey Finns, von Einem could do whatever he liked. Invariably, they would have a sore bum at the end of the saga. Sometimes they would have a tear in their anus, like George, the hitchhiker.

These actions, however, didn't show that von Einem killed boys. The boys were released from von Einem's control and sent home. The sending of the boys home, in fact, helped prove that he wasn't a killer — rather, the opposite. The fact that von Einem picked up boys, drugged them and abused them did not mean that he forcibly grabbed Richard Kelvin and drugged and abused him before killing him. However, history has shown that a man does not sexually abuse every woman he picks up even though he might be a serial rapist. Just in the same way, a killer does not murder every person he meets. Von Einem could fit into this situation, in which he picked up some boys, let some go, spiked the drinks of others and abused them, then let them go. However, it was possible there were a few that he did not let go. It was possible that he killed them.

The other boys could give evidence that they were picked up by a helpful stranger who they could identify as von Einem. Again, this does not prove that von Einem would forcibly drag someone into a car but the evidence against him was starting to build. With many police investigations, once the arrest occurs the case gets stronger and stronger. With von Einem it was no different.

When the employees at von Einem's work were interviewed, all of them said that they knew or suspected he was a homosexual. Some thought he was harmless, while others thought he was a bit off, especially when he used to perv at the young men on the Coca-Cola truck who delivered drinks to the work site.

One of the employees at von Einem's work told of an episode which clearly demonstrated just how much von Einem couldn't help himself. The co-worker found von Einem in the warehouse one weekend. Once again he was with a young boy and they were in von Einem's car. It was between the time he was first spoken to by us in July and before he was arrested on 3 November 1983. He was continuing to pick up young boys even though he knew the police were interested in him.

One of the female employees at Pipeline Supplies of Australia went regularly to the Mars Bar in Gouger Street and was supplied drugs by von Einem. She knew that he picked up boys. The woman told about the time that von Einem met her at one of the pie carts in the city. Pie carts are an Adelaide institution; caravans would come into the city at night to serve hot food such as pies, pasties and soup to late-night revellers. Von Einem had a boy with him. He rushed towards her and put his arm around her neck and whispered in her ear.

'There you are. I've been looking for you,' von Einem said to his work colleague. 'Pretend you are my wife. I've told the kid you are my wife and I've been looking for you.'

One time she asked him about a boy that she helped him pick up.

'What did you do with the lad?'

'Oh, I just took him home and let him sleep it off.'

Then von Einem embellished his story.

'Oh, when I got him there I hit him up in the foot because not many look for injection holes in people's feet and then I fist fucked him and I used surgical instruments and put them up his anus.'

This information from the work colleague of von Einem occurred after I left Major Crime and, when I read her statement years later, memories came flooding back.

Injection sites. Ross James, the pathologist, thought there may have been an injection site in Richard's arm but he couldn't be sure. There was a suggestion of Rohypnol in Richard's system but the forensic scientists couldn't be sure about that either but Rohypnol, however, was one of von Einem's drugs of choice when abusing boys. I remembered members of the team searching for snuff movies and them finding the video Fist Fuckers of America *— all about placing a fist in someone's anus.*

He was also telling the woman who worked with him about placing surgical instruments up the boy's anus and I vividly recalled B, the young deviate, drawing pictures of the torch and crochet needle he saw von Einem putting up the anus of the drugged hitchhiker.

We had the evidence of B who told about von Einem's potential for violence when one of the drugged boys in his unit was waking up. The words were pretty blunt: 'Bevan said that he would kill the cunt if he woke up.' Legally, this didn't prove von Einem was a murderer — far from it. The words were hearsay and there are strong rules of evidence to prevent hearsay being admitted in a criminal trial. But the words did indicate that the man had a disposition towards violence.

Von Einem denied knowing or having anything to do with Richard Kelvin when he was first interviewed on 28 July 1983. However, even with all of this information, our case was still lacking, as the disappearance of Richard Kelvin was different. He wasn't picked up like the others — in the sense that he went voluntarily. He was abducted.

We knew Richard was abducted because on the Tuesday after he went missing we found our first witness saying that he heard cries for help and a car speeding away. Since that time we had found other witnesses who heard Richard's abduction, with its loud noises, the crying out and car doors banging before the car sped away. The witnesses varied in their stories and that was not unusual. People see and hear things differently but from what they told us we knew that at least two and possibly as many as four people abducted Richard. Also, a high-pitched voice was heard by one of the witnesses — that high-pitched voice could have been a woman's voice. We now suspected that von Einem used women or transvestites to pick up boys, so one of his female associates could have been involved. So, we had a group of abductors with a woman or a transvestite possibly being involved.

But what actually happened on this occasion? What caused Richard to be snatched in such a savage way when other boys had been wooed so calmly and easily. More than likely the mix of people who were involved was different from usual and that combination caused them to act differently. We knew that von Einem had a beat, which involved driving between the city and Scotty's Motel looking for hitchhikers. He would do this alone or with another person. We knew that von Einem and B would pick up hitchhikers and offer them drugs or spike their drinks. We also believed von Einem used transsexuals and transvestites. A man and a woman in a car would be less threatening to hitchhikers than two men in a car.

Richard Kelvin, however, was different. He was not seduced into a car, he was physically forced into one.

In my mind, the dog collar was the catalyst. Richard Kelvin was a young, fit boy and would have been attractive to homosexuals. Normally, homosexuals would not approach him because they would sense his distaste for homosexuality, but when a group gets together, people act differently. They can form a pack that roams together. Whether or not the pack comprises men or women, they can behave more aggressively in some situations than if they were alone. When von Einem was by himself he appeared gentle — until he had people under his control.

Control of people who became von Einem's prey was achieved through drugs. On that Sunday night he was not alone, and, rather than being with just one other person, he was probably with two or three others. That number of people would be needed to force someone into a car. As police officers, we know just how hard it is to put an arrested person into a police car if that person does not want to get in.

It was a weekend and most likely they had drugs in their system. The drugs may have been alcohol, hypnotics or marijuana but most likely it was a combination of drugs. Either they were getting over them from their use on the weekend or they had come together and taken a fresh lot. This pack was out to play and when they had finished socialising they were ready to hunt for their prey. They were using von Einem's beat, which included North Adelaide. They knew people would be going to the restaurants and shops at six o'clock on a Sunday night. Unfortunately, fate put Richard Kelvin in the vicinity of this pack as they cruised O'Connell Street and the dog collar Richard wore that night activated their 'smell of blood'. From then on their hunt was uncontrollable.

Brian Martin, the senior crown prosecutor, couldn't prove this, though. The scenario was very likely but prosecutors have to present evidence that is acceptable to courts. Supposition was not enough. Brian was intending to present to the court people who had been picked up by von Einem and drugged and abused by him. But he knew there would be difficulties with a legal concept which relates to that specific type of evidence. The type of evidence is called circumstantial, and the legal concept was called similar fact evidence. Our case relied on evidence which suggested that von Einem was with Richard Kelvin and evidence from witnesses saying that Richard would not go with strangers.

Brian Martin was going to introduce evidence to show that von Einem acted in such a way that a jury could conclude that he was the person who picked up Richard Kelvin. He could prove that von Einem picked up boys and drugged them with the same type of drugs that were found in Richard Kelvin. The boys we found were either given a Mickey Finn or they took the drugs voluntarily, for kicks.

However, the majority of the boys we found were given Rohypnol but we couldn't prove that Richard had been given that particular drug. This presented additional problems. George, the hitchhiker, on the other hand, was given Mandrax, and that was the same drug given to Richard Kelvin.

Richard Kelvin would not have taken the drugs voluntarily, but they may have been in drinks that he was given. There were similarities there. Richard Kelvin was anally abused. This fact presented similarities with other boys. Richard Kelvin was beaten during his captivity and other boys who gave us statements about von Einem were not beaten. This presented differences, which a defence team could use; perhaps the bruises on his body resulted from his being beaten to make him take the drugs, but this was all speculation.

The differences between the boys who were drugged, abused and let go and Richard Kelvin, were going to present difficulties for Brian Martin. Our evidence of similar acts was weak, but he was going to try. The law of evidence was strict and Brian would have to use all of his persuasive skills to get that evidence accepted by a judge in a court. However, to a lay person, von Einem's actions showed he was a person who picked up, drugged and abused boys. That makes him a very good suspect to be a person who picked up, drugged, abused and killed boys.

We had a boy who was abducted on a Sunday. That was 5 June 1983. We could show that he was probably dumped on a Sunday. That was 10 July 1983. The findings of the Maggot Lady and the pathologist showed that the boy was probably killed between 8 and 10 July 1983 and dumped at the airstrip on Sunday, 10 July 1983. A man who was walking his dogs on the airstrip on the Sunday said that

Richard's body wasn't there earlier during the Sunday. He had four terrier dogs, with two younger ones on a lead whilst the other two were allowed to move through the bush. The dogs and their owner walked in the area where Richard was laid on the ground. If he was there when they were walking, then he would have been found. Also, the weather conditions and the growth cycle of the fly's larvae showed that he couldn't have been dumped after the 10th. He had to have been disposed of late on that Sunday.

So with Richard Kelvin, Sunday keeps coming into the picture. He was abducted on a Sunday and he was dumped on a Sunday. This fitted with our original theories about our murderers being working people who plied their deadly trade mainly on weekends. However, they were opportunists, and they were active on other days but were freer to hunt their prey on weekends.

Richard was kept alive for five weeks after his abduction. We could prove all of these things. We knew that Richard Kelvin was drugged and beaten during his captivity but Richard would not have been completely out to it. He still had to drink to stay alive. We could show that he had eaten food at some time during his captivity as he had food in his stomach. He had eaten an apple and cornflakes just before his death. But we still could not be certain about the cause of death. Richard could have died from his anal injury but suffocation could not be discounted.

So this was the sum of the case so far: We had an admitted homosexual who picked up boys. We could prove that he also drugged boys. He worked in an office and had weekends off. We found drugs hidden in his house that were similar to those Richard had in his system. Richard had Mandrax in his system. Mandrax was found hidden in von Einem's house. He also had trichloroethanol in his system, which is the byproduct of having been given chloral hydrate, the active ingredient of the drug, Noctec, which was also found hidden in von Einem's house. He also had the active ingredient of Valium, diazepam, in his system. Additionally, there was a suspicion that Rohypnol was also present in Richard but the amount could not be measured. This also presented problems as to whether or not that evidence would be accepted. Even so, von Einem also had quantities of Rohypnol in his pill bottle in his bag. We knew that he used Rohypnol to drug boys. Valium tablets also were found in his little pill bottle with the piece of paper with 'Uncle Bevan' written on it.

How sickly ironic were those words, I pondered. The doctor or person who wrote 'Uncle Bevan' and placed those words in his drug bottle knew von Einem gave the appearance of being a nice, 'uncle' figure. In reality he was a shocking deviate.

Another problem related to the fourth drug. A barbiturate was also found in Richard's system but we did not find any at von Einem's. However, we knew others were involved and they could have been drug users. Brian Martin could argue that one of the other killers supplied the barbiturates.

Not only did the evidence of von Einem picking up and drugging boys become more clear as time passed, but other circumstantial evidence became stronger. That evidence related to miniscule particles found on Richard's clothing. Des

Phillips took fibre samples from von Einem's house when we first went there on 28 July 1983. Also, von Einem volunteered a sample of his hair, which was taken by police doctor Noel McCleave on the same day. When Des had dried Richard's jeans, socks and T-shirt and taken tape lifts from them, he found trace evidence: sand, paint, fibres and hair.

The sand from Richard's clothes was quite fine and it was subsequently looked at by AMDEL, a centre which examines minerals — but nothing came from this line of enquiry. The sand was quite common and we couldn't determine where it came from.

Small particles of paint were found, which was predominantly coloured red. There were forty small fragments, which was quite a large amount. Beneath the paint there appeared to be a yellow undercoat, possibly a metal primer, but we could not be sure. The size of the largest chip of paint found by Des Phillips was half a millimetre. This chip was a light green colour and was similar to paint found on Mark Langley. Other coloured paint flakes were four particles showing different green colours: particles of grey paint, blue paint and yellow paint. Unfortunately, we couldn't match any of the paint with the colours at the homes we visited.

There were 525 foreign fibres on Richard's clothes and they were sorted into their different colours: mainly red, orange, brown, violet and aqua. The red fibres were mostly synthetic but there were some woollen fibres. The orange fibres were a combination of synthetic and wool, and most of the foreign fibres were taken from Richard's jeans. The brown fibres were predominantly wool but some were synthetic, while the violet fibres were synthetic and all over Richard's clothing; the aqua fibres were also synthetic.

The scientific evidence to show that Richard Kelvin was at von Einem's home was standing up to scrutiny. At the time of von Einem's arrest the fibre evidence was still being checked. Scientific examination using a technique called thin-layer chromatography showed that nine different coloured fibres from four different sources — all relating to von Einem — were on all of Richard Kelvin's clothes, including his underpants. There were blue and turquoise fibres that were exactly the same as fibres from von Einem's bedroom carpet; blue and purple fibres that were exactly the same as fibres in his passageway and loungeroom; and yellow and orange fibres from the bedspread in his bedroom.

Of the 525 fibres recovered from Richard's clothing, 196 were from von Einem's home or his clothing. Thirty-eight came from his bedspread, twenty-seven came from his bedroom carpet, twenty-one from his hall and lounge carpet, and 110 fibres found on Richard were from von Einem's brown cardigan. Only two fibres from Richard's own home environment were left on his clothing. No fibres from the maroon velour seats of von Einem's Toyota Corona hatchback were on Richard's clothes. There could be no doubt that von Einem was with Richard and, with the number of fibres from von Einem's cardigan, it showed close contact.

Many hairs were found on Richard's clothing and while most of them were Richard's, there were a number of hairs from a different source. Five of von Einem's head hairs were found inside Richard's jeans. The interesting thing about von Einem's hair was that it had no medulla or central core, which gives hair its colour. The lack of pigmentation could be seen at the base of the hair while the top section was dyed.

The dye was a combination of N2 Schwarzkopf and Ingora Royal applied by the second person von Einem nominated as one of his best friends. He was a male hairdresser who had the nickname 'Pussy'. He dyed von Einem's hair once a month because von Einem had been greying since he was sixteen. On Monday, 6 June 1983, the day after Richard Kelvin went missing, von Einem had his hair dyed just before his hairdresser friend went to Melbourne on holidays. The hair samples from von Einem were found to be indistinguishable from the dyed hair found on Richard's clothing. In other words, the hair was the same and the dye on the hair was the same.

Scientific evidence, of course, can be problematic. While the search for the serial killers who murdered the boys was going on, a Royal Commission was considering the scientific evidence in another murder case — the murder of Rosa Simper. This case caused Des and Ivan and the forensic scientists to be very careful with their tests and conclusions from the evidence they had collected.

Rosa Simper was a seventy-seven year-old lady living alone at Woodville in the western suburbs of Adelaide. She had been sexually assaulted and viciously strangled with her brassiere during the early hours of 3 December 1977. An iron bar was inserted into her anus and vagina before her house was ransacked. Two hundred dollars worth of property was stolen.

Crime scene examiners vacuumed the sheets of the bed where she was murdered and found microscopic evidence. Microscopic particles of wood, foam, fibres, paint and metal were found and taken for examination. Paint and metal were also found on the window ledge where the murderer entered the house at about two in the morning. This trace evidence provided the evidence that was used to convict Edward Splatt.

John McCall from the Major Crime Squad led the Simper murder investigation. John was a short and nuggetty detective who drank and smoked — not big drinks like some detectives but he could sip away for hours, reflecting on cases. He had been in the Squad for years and was in the Homicide Squad prior to that. John was very experienced and very competent at investigating murders.

As paint and metal were found at the home and, in particular, on the sheet where Mrs Simper was sleeping, similar to paint and metal used in the Wilson's factory across the road about sixty metres from the house, John concentrated his investigations there. However, all of the factory workers had traces of metal and paint on their clothes so crime scene examiners searched for differentiating trace evidence.

Edward Charles Splatt, who was a spray painter at the factory, was arrested because police and forensic scientist believed trace evidence found at the Simper home came from Splatt and that there was circumstantial evidence to prove that Splatt murdered Rosa Simper. However, over time these beliefs were show to be incorrectly based.

An *Advertiser* newspaper story questioned the guilt of Edward Splatt and sufficient pressure was brought on the government to have a Royal Commission into the evidence presented at the trial. The Commission sat for 196 days and finished in March 1984, three months before Richard disappeared. The Royal Commissioner handed down his finding and said that the additional scientific evidence that was produced during the Commission 'cast doubt on the validity of the jury's verdict'. Edward Splatt was released from jail and given $300,000 from the government.

The Royal Commission questioned the validity of the scientific evidence because assumptions were made by one of the crime scene examiners and by a forensic scientist. The findings from the Royal Commission made police crime scene examiners and forensic scientists very careful and wary when presenting their evidence in court; all of this was happening while we were investigating the murder of five boys. We couldn't afford for such evidence to be criticised again as it would affect our case and the credibility of the whole justice system would be open to attack.

When trace materials are used in evidence, the prosecution must show three things, which are that: the trace evidence was found where it was said to be found; the trace materials, which link the victim to the murderer, must come from the same source; and the accused was so closely in contact with the victim that he must have committed the murder.

These comments of the Royal Commissioner confirmed past court judgments and these three points had to be covered in any trial using the finding of trace evidence.

Crime scene examiners and forensic scientists had been severely criticised in the Royal Commission. This provided opportunities for the defence to criticise our case.

Barry Jennings was now assisting Helena Jasinski with the defence of von Einem. They were told about the evidence concerning the drugs, fibre and hair prior to the committal. They checked the evidence with their own experts, and also checked the reputation of the people who were presenting the evidence. They had the criticisms of the Splatt Royal Commission to use as a guide. Von Einem said that he was not with Richard Kelvin but the hairs and fibres told us differently. Richard Kelvin was at von Einem's house at some stage but that was a long way from proving abduction and murder. Also, von Einem had the opportunity and the pills to pick up and control Richard Kelvin.

Von Einem didn't have to say anything and we would have been presenting a circumstantial case to the jury because no one could say that they saw him with Richard Kelvin at any stage. But the trace evidence presented strong circumstantial evidence to show that Richard was with von Einem. That, with the drugs and similar fact evidence of the drugged boys, presented a good case but there's nothing like a witness to tell the jury what really happened. So far we didn't have one. As well, Brian Martin and Paul Rofe were concerned because the public and potential jurors would be aware of problems with scientific evidence because of the Splatt Royal Commission.

❂ ❂ ❂

The committal to determine whether or not there was enough evidence to send von Einem for trial started on 20 February 1984. There was an adjournment after the first day and it restarted on 27 February 1984. Barry Jennings and Helena Jasinski knew that they didn't have to say anything at this stage. The committal was an opportunity for the defence to test the prosecution case.

Things started to get interesting on the 28th. Barry Jennings said to the court that he had instructions from his client, von Einem.

'Your Honour, my instructions are that on the night of Sunday, 5 June 1983, Richard Kelvin was willingly in the company of the defendant and that he had a conversation with the defendant in the course of which he mentioned *inter alia* the fact that, paraphrasing and putting this in broad terms, that he had problems at school and was ragged. This was something he was upset about.'

Von Einem wanted to say that he was with Richard Kelvin. This was sensational news and a fantastic development. This statement showed our scientific evidence was right and now we should have less concerns about presenting it in court.

Barry and Helena advised him not to say anything but von Einem had wanted to provide an explanation about why his hair and fibres from his house and cardigan were on Richard's clothes. Von Einem thought he was smarter than the system. He thought he could beat the system, perhaps, just as he had done previously. But judgment day was fast approaching — we would have to wait and see just how smart this deviate really was.

Chapter 11

The Alibi

Trevor and I drove down Port Road, which leads to Port Adelaide and Mutton Cove. At Thebarton, we turned the police car right to the appropriately named Gaol Road. We drove past the police barracks. The famous police greys trotted in their paddocks amongst the olive trees and we continued on to the remand jail where von Einem was being held. The new remand centre had not yet been completed and prisoners waiting to go to court were kept at the old Adelaide Jail. The first sections of the old Adelaide Jail were completed by 1841, five years after the State was founded, and it was the first government building of the colony of South Australia.

We parked out the front and met Helena Jasinski, who was standing by the side of her car waiting for us.

I wonder how von Einem found you? I thought. Lawyers don't generally advertise so people don't really know where to go. People who are involved in the court system want the best lawyer they can afford but where do you find a good criminal lawyer who is going to get you off? Legal aid lawyers are found through the system but when a lawyer is not working for legal aid, how are they found? Invariably, people must talk and lawyers' names get passed around. She had been fair and reasonable in her dealing with Trevor and I previously, and I wondered what would happen on this occasion.

Together we moved towards the archway that held the two large wooden doors of the jail. Of all the times that I have been to the jail and run past it during various training courses at the Thebarton Police Barracks, I have never seen those two massive gates open. What does open is a much smaller rectangular door cut into the arched gate on the right side. A peephole is cut in the left-hand gate for jailers to see who is there.

After approaching the doors, Trevor pressed the buzzer. A fat face peered at us inquiringly through the peephole.

'We're here to speak to Bevan von Einem,' Trevor said.

The face looked at the three of us without emotion and the keys jangled on the large stainless steel ring attached to the man's belt. Metal hit metal and the large key turned in the lock of the access door. The guard swung open the door.

We stepped down into the sallyport of the jail. The roadway leading to the gates had been built up with layers of bitumen and now the roadway was higher than the green concrete floor immediately behind the doors. We entered the four metre by ten metre reception area of the jail; a glass and wood office which would have been built in the 1960s sat inside the sallyport. It took up a quarter of the area and provided some comfort for the jailers. There were also offices either side of the rectangular area. Access to the inner sanctum of the jail was stopped by two gates made of iron rod and bars mounted on the other side of the sallyport. They also were arched and the same size as the front gates but made of metal.

I stood with the metal bars rising up in front of me and I looked through them to the circle yard on the other side of the arched iron gates. When horses and carts were used, the circle yard allowed prison vans and carts to enter the jail, circle round and head back out. Now motor vehicles are used, the yard was filled with a fibro building, which allowed prisoners and their families to talk but not have physical contact. It was appropriately called the visitors' non-contact building. The whole place was cold and forbidding.

A prison warder pointed to the visitor's book lying on a sloping shelf near the left-hand iron gate.

'Fill out the book.'

We all signed the entrance book, giving our names, addresses and reason for being at the jail. We all gave our business addresses.

'Just a moment and we will have someone take you to the interview room.'

Trevor had rung previously to make sure that von Einem would be available. He wanted to make sure that he wasn't involved in some jail activity that he couldn't quickly be taken from. We didn't want to wait around any longer than necessary in this place.

The jailer's key opened the iron access gate built into the grill of the inner right-hand metal gate. He showed us to the interview rooms in the painted stone building immediately to the right of the circle yard, next to the visitors building. The rectangular building with fifty centimetre-thick stone walls was one of the oldest buildings in the jail, built in 1841 and originally a cell block. Its age was evident by the yellow paint flaking off the stone at the bottom of the walls, showing the white crystal which indicated rising damp.

The two tiny rooms closest to us were the interview rooms for solicitors and police. The second room was the largest and, even so, it was only three metres by 1.5 metres. We headed for it. There weren't any windows and, while some light came in through two glass sections in the vented door, we still had to turn on the single fluoro to provide sufficient light. The walls of the room were painted the same yellow colour as the outside ones, and blended with the grey lino tiles. There were three chairs in the room scattered around a wooden desk. An old Remington typewriter sat on top. I found another chair from the room next door and brought it back. Trevor had bought a folder with foolscap paper and carbon for the interview.

A smaller man than the first brought von Einem to the room. He was the same as before — emotionless and bland — there was no obvious personality.

Trevor sat at the desk, his back to the door, facing the typewriter. Helena and von Einem were on the other side of him, their chairs pushed back to provide space between the desk and their bodies. I sat next to Trevor, facing the corner of the table with my chair also pushed back as much as possible in the compressed space.

Trevor started the interview with von Einem. He typed his own words on the paper rolled into the typewriter before he asked his first question.

'Did you see Richard Kelvin on the evening of Sunday, 5th June 1983?'

'I did.'

'Would you tell me in your own words how you came to see him and what happened?'

'I arrived in North Adelaide from my home with the intention of buying my tea at one of the fish and chip shops there in O'Connell Street. I pulled in to park the car but there were no vacant spaces on either side of the road. I drove to the lights and turned left into Ward Street and left again into ... I don't know the name of the street, do you want me to go on?'

'Yes, without the map at this stage if you wouldn't mind.'

'A lad ran from a side street on my left, across the street in front of the car. I braked and stopped and wound my window down and told this person that he was lucky I didn't run into him. He approached my door resting his two arms on the roof.'

Von Einem then showed Trevor how Richard Kelvin rested his arms on the roof of his car. He demonstrated with his hands together and elbows out.

I kept a straight face while thinking to myself: *Yeah, you bastard, you are just trying to cover your tracks. When you dragged Richard into the car, he would have put his hands on the roof to try and stop himself being pushed and dragged into the car.* I tried not to show any emotion in my face.

Von Einem continued.

'I was drinking a can of beer. He asked me for a drink. I didn't offer him a drink. I asked him his age and he told me sixteen. I said that he could hop in the car if he wanted a drink but not in the street, to drink out of the can that is. He got in the car and I drove up the street to Archer Street and turned right into Archer Street and asked him if he wanted to drive around and he said "Yes".'

I don't get elated very often but a wave of relief washed through my body at this point. My face and body did not show it, I hope, but I was elated. Von Einem had blown it. Our concerns about problems with juries and scientific evidence were over.

As that wave of excitment passed through my body, Trevor impassively continued to ask questions of von Einem. My partner's body language did not give anything away but I knew what he was thinking.

Great! Great! Just keep talking. You think you're smart enough to get away with murder. You're not as smart as you think.

Von Einem continued to tell his story about how Richard Kelvin told him that he was having trouble at school and trouble with skinheads.

Yes, this is all information that was in the newspapers, I thought to myself. *You would have picked up this information from the media after he went missing.*

He then said that he took Richard Kelvin to his home at Paradise.

'He came in the front door into the passage, walked into the lounge and sat on the long lounge, the settee. In the lounge room he kicked his shoes off. I can't recall whether he put his shoes on to walk elsewhere or not. From the lounge, he turned right into the passage and left down the passage to my bedroom. He sat on the bed, [walked] back into the lounge room the same way, then leaving the same way as he came, through the front door.'

Later during the interview von Einem said: 'The conversation would have got around to hobbies but I can't recall what he did as a hobby.'

No, you can't say about his hobbies because you don't know about them. Nothing was in the papers about his hobbies.

'I mentioned my harp to him and that I had one and we went into my bedroom where I showed him the instrument. We sat on the bed; I played the harp . . .'

Yes, more lies to explain how fibres from your bedspread and bedroom carpet were on Richard Kelvin's clothes. What fifteen-year-old boy would go with a stranger to his home to listen to him play his harp in his bedroom?

'While Richard was at your place did you touch each other at all?'

'Yes.'

'To what extent exactly, repeat exactly, did you touch each other?'

'I put my arm around him as he was upset with his friends he was having problems with.'

Now he is trying to explain how fibres from his cardigan were on Richard's clothes.

'How upset was he about the matter?'

'He was fairly upset.'

'Crying?'

'He could have been crying, yes.'

Anything you are asked that you had not thought about before, you are vague with your answer. You were definite about how Richard's hands were on your car.

'Was he crying or not?'

'Well, from what I can recall he was sniffling.'

He finally said that he spent two hours at his home with Richard Kelvin before he took him back into town and dropped him off at the Palais car park opposite the Royal Adelaide Hospital. Von Einem said he gave him $20 to catch one of the taxis parked outside the hospital.

Yes, you like giving money to boys to get them home in taxis. Just like you did with the hitchhiker, George. But Richard never made it home.

When he was first interviewed on 28 July 1983, four days after Richard's disappearance, von Einem denied any personal contact with Richard. Trevor asked questions about this.

'You have during earlier interviews told some untruths then, is this right?'

'Yes.'

'From memory now, what parts were untruths?'

'My mother was not at home. I also said that he [Richard Kelvin] was not in my home.'

So, eight months after he first denied knowing anything about Richard Kelvin and part-way through the preliminary hearing, he changed his story. Von Einem was trying to give an alibi to us at the Adelaide Jail. Von Einem now said that Richard voluntarily got in his car, he happily went for a drive with him and spent two hours with him at his home before he was dropped off at North Terrace and given $20.

Trevor continued the interview.

'Did he give you any indication that he was a homosexual or bisexual?'

'His appearance gave me the impression that he could have been bisexual.'

'What gave you that impression?'

'By his actions.'

'What actions?'

'The way he spoke.'

'Is that all?'

'Yes.'

That didn't work. Trevor was trying to get him to talk about the dog collar. If von Einem admitted that he saw the dog collar then he could show that he was lying during this interview as well. We knew that Boris got him to take the dog collar off at the bus stop. If von Einem said that he saw the dog collar, then he must have seen it in O'Connell Street or later whilst he held him captive and put the dog collar back on him.

'Richard was physically abducted from the North Adelaide area, wasn't he?'

'No,' von Einem replied.

'Where was your mother on that evening, the 5th June?'

'My mother was at her cousin[s]' at Houghton.'

'What name?'

'Alcorn.'

'Christian names?'

'Beryl and Ken.'

'When did she go there?'

'Saturday afternoon.'

Trevor asked about the booze von Einem kept in his car. He had already told us he was drinking beer and we knew he used to put drugs in the alcohol to seduce the boys.

'Where was your esky?'

By this time Trevor knew that von Einem would drive around with an esky full of drinks in his car.

'On the backseat.'

'Did you have much alcohol in it?'

'Well it had alcohol in it but I didn't go out on the Saturday night for entertainment because I locked myself out of the house and had to go to see my mother to get her key.'

So, that's what he calls his activities — entertainment.

'You are aware that your mother told us you were home at about 6 p.m. on Sunday 5th. Why did she say that, do you know?'

'On the spur of the moment. She probably wouldn't remember what she did on that particular date because she does visit her cousin, I don't know how often, but at regular intervals she stays up there.'

'Alcorn's house is pretty close to the airstrip where Richard's body was located, isn't it?'

'Er, yes.'

Later in the interview Trevor asked questions about von Einem telling lies when we spoke to him in July.

'I'll ask you again. Why didn't you speak up about all of this earlier?'

'When he was reported missing I thought that he had run away from home and that he would turn up. I didn't want my family, mainly my mother, to know that I did have him at home. I regret not speaking up as I could not foresee into the future and what eventually happened to him.'

Trevor continued the interview because he wanted to check this alibi. Also, we believed that Richard had been kept at other places during the five weeks of his captivity.

'Now, a last word or two about your movements in relation to Sunday 5th. You told us you returned home after dropping Richard off at North Terrace. Did you stay home for the rest of the evening?'

'No.'

'What did you do then?'

'I went to my sister's house at Campbelltown with the intention to get her to pick up Mum because it was about elevenish. I didn't go in because I couldn't really expect my sister to drive up there at that time of night to pick my mother up, so I rang my mother from a phone box around the corner from my sister's and spoke with my mother and said I would come up the following morning, tomorrow morning, and pick her up.'

'Did you in fact do that? If so, what vehicle did you use?'

'Are you referring to Monday?'

'Sunday night. You said you phoned your mother and agreed to pick her up the next day.'

'Monday.'

'Yes.'

'I did not pick her up.'

'What is your story there, then?'

'My sister came to my place at about 9.30 a.m. She normally comes to visit my mother. I wasn't well.'

Von Einem then told how he was sick with the 'flu all of that week and got a doctor's certificate from his local doctor at Campbelltown during the week. He went back to work a week later, on the Tuesday, the day after a public holiday. Trevor asked von Einem what he did the weekend after Richard went missing.

'I stayed home Saturday and Sunday until Sunday night. I went out Sunday night and I drove to the airport. On my way home from the airport I gave two hitchhikers a lift. We got into town and they were not doing anything in particular so I asked them if they would like a drink and as they said they weren't doing anything in particular and it was a long weekend, I suggested that we go to my friend's place, which was [the home of one of von Einem's close associates]. At that stage I had a key to the flat. When we arrived there [he] was not home and we went inside and [he] arrived about five minutes after us. He opened some beer and we had a drink and we rang [the businessman] to come over and [he] came approximately half an hour later. We drank beer, they stayed the night. I left there about 1.30 ...'

Well, he's prepared to mention his friends to cover his activities. He might have something over them to make sure they say the right thing.

'Did anyone have sex with the hitchhikers at [the male prostitute's] flat?'

'[The businessman] said he did but I didn't know.'

Von Einem took about 25 minutes to read the record of interview that Trevor typed. Both he and Helena signed the document. Trevor and I signed the bottom of each page, then von Einem left the interview room to go to dinner. Helena, Trevor and I walked from the jail and Helena got into her car to drive off.

Trevor and I started talking excitedly as we walked out through those big wooden doors of the Adelaide Jail and moved towards our police car away from Helena's hearing. Quietly but quickly we spoke about the interview.

'What did you think about that?'

'What about when he said that he picked up Richard? You beauty!'

The case against von Einem continued to get stronger. The discovery of Mandrax in Richard Kelvin and Mark Langley was the first break. Finding the script for Mandrax with von Einem's name on it was the second. The hair and fibres was the third break. This was the fourth.

We got into the police car and drove back to the office. As we turned into Port Road, Trevor laughed — not his big belly laugh but a quieter laugh reflecting his happiness and understanding of what had happened.

Chapter 12

The Trial

Over a year after Richard disappeared, the trial against Bevan Spencer von Einem began on Monday, 15 October 1984. Six months had passed since the committal and von Einem's incredible revelations of how he picked up Richard Kelvin. For the police it was largely a matter of tidying up the paperwork and following up detail for the prosecutors. As the start of the trial came closer and closer, Brian Martin and Paul Rofe were putting in the hours making sure they had the information they needed. They were now in charge of the case and Trevor and I were subservient to them.

There was an enormous amount of interest in the case. Murders naturally generate attention and when the trial was about the abduction, abuse and murder of a young boy the interest escalated, especially after four other young men had been abused and killed over the previous four years. On top of this, the young boy was the son of a popular television newsreader. The events had a huge following.

During the whole period of the trial, spectators filed into the Supreme Court building of South Australia. The Sir Samuel Way Building is unusual as this formal and ornate structure was not originally built to be a court. The building was formerly a department store, modelled on the Galleries Lafayette store in Paris. It opened as the department store, 'Charles Moore', in 1912 but the store closed in 1980 and was redesigned as a court building. The architects retained the building's façade and kept its grand marble staircase, which was rebuilt under a central atrium.

The trial was conducted in the largest courtroom, on the western side of the building. To get to it visitors walked up the massive central staircase and headed to the rear right of the building. Court Number Eight was one of the two largest courtrooms in the building. Trevor and I walked up and down that staircase many times over the following weeks.

The floor of the large square room was covered with rich gold carpet, spreading to the wood panelling that reached about one and a half metres up the walls. Mellow yellow paint flowed upwards to the high ceilings and downlights, which directed light onto wooden desks and carpet while recessed lights were hidden high up in the walls. The richness of the room provided the proceedings with an extra sense of importance.

Justice White, of the Supreme Court, presided over the case, and he sat on the one chair behind the largest desk in the room. The bench stretched almost across the full width of the room. In front of the judge's desk was another one about half the size and the judge's associate, clerk of court and stenographer sat behind it. The courtroom's design reinforced society's hierarchy — the judge being the most important person in the room. We hoped his views would consider the prosecution case in a positive way, but you could never be sure.

Two rectangular stalls were built against the walls on both sides of the room and each enclosure contained seating for twelve people. The box on the right contained seats for the jury, which would soon contain twelve people from the community while the box on the left allowed up to twelve accused to sit in it. But only one person would fill that box. Trevor and I would have liked more in there but it wasn't to be.

In the middle of the room another large rectangular desk covered the plush carpet. The defence counsel sat on the left of the table and the two prosecutors sat on the right. Behind them two curved rows of seating spread across the room for additional solicitors and support staff. The remaining area of the court at the rear provided seating for 100 people in five rows of seats. They filled on the first day and continued to be busy with people over the next fifteen days.

The trial started with the selection of the jury. Fifty people picked from the electoral roll were selected for one month's jury service. They entered the room and sat in the public gallery. The judge, prosecution and defence counsel all had lists of the names of these potential jurors. Brian Martin, Queen's Counsel, who would lead the prosecution case for the D.P.P.'s office, read out the list of witnesses who would be called during the trial and the potential jurors were asked to leave the room if they knew any of the witnesses. Two stood up and moved towards the Sheriff's Officer to have the opportunity to be selected for another trial.

The clerk of the court read out names of the potential jurors and one by one they stood up and moved from the body of the court to the juror's box. The defence and prosecution counsel each have an opportunity to refuse three people without giving any reasons. The process finished quickly and the twelve seats in the jurors' box filled. Over the coming days, the seven women and five men found their preferred positions in the jury box, where they were as comfortable as they could be as jurors in the murder trial of one person accused of killing another.

Brian Martin addressed the jury to open the trial. Paul Rofe supported him. Brian started putting the jigsaw together, which, when complete, would provide a picture of the prosecution case. He addressed them at the start of the trial by giving a description of the evidence that he would be piecing together.

Helena Jasinski briefed Barry Jennings and together they defended von Einem. Barry was a smaller man than the two prosecutors and completely different in appearance. His black curly hair spread out over his head and surrounded his glasses. He was a prosecutor before he went into private practice and knew the tactics that Brian and Paul would employ.

Brian Martin emphasised that von Einem committed Richard Kelvin's murder with other people. By saying he did not act alone, the easiest scenario for the jury to accept was presented. It would have been difficult for one person to keep Richard captive for five weeks, especially when von Einem was at work from the second week of the disappearance. He wasn't with Richard for all of the time he was kept captive. Also, there was the evidence from witnesses that more than one person was heard when Richard was grabbed at the corner of Margaret and Ward Streets, North Adelaide.

Another point that Brian Martin made during the trial was that the actual cause of death could not be known for certain. Ross James, the pathologist, could say that Richard Kelvin didn't die from natural causes. All of Richard's vital organs were healthy. He could say that the beatings did not cause Richard to die. The subdural haematoma, where blood gathered between the skull and brain, was life threatening but he survived that injury. Also, although the anal injury to Richard caused massive bleeding and shock, it could never be proved that it actually caused his death. We always believed that was possible, but Ross could not discount other possible causes of death: for example, he could not discount the possibility that Richard was suffocated.

The Crown case involved proving different points. Firstly, murder would be proved by showing Richard was forcibly abducted, he had been injured and heavily drugged during his captivity and he had no defensive injuries.

Proving von Einem was implicated in the murder would be shown by the facts that: von Einem had the opportunity; he had access to the necessary drugs; he had been away from work during the first week of Richard's disappearance, which provided him an opportunity to help keep Richard captive; he sold his car six days after Richard Kelvin was dumped, and he repainted most of his boot before it was sold, indicating that he had something to hide; scientific evidence would show that von Einem was with Richard Kelvin in his home; and he had denied being with Richard.

Brian called his first witness. It was Marty White, a tall, greying policeman who did scale drawings of various locations. Brian used Marty to present diagrams of different locations so the jury could refer to them during the trial. He presented and explained the scale drawings he made of the Kelvin home, the route to the bus stop, plans of the inside of the homes of witnesses, plans of von Einem's home and of all the locations that were going to be talked about during the trial. The opening address and tendering of documents and plans completed the first day.

The next day the court did not sit inside the Sir Samuel Way Building but moved to the various locations that were to be talked about during the trial. The jury was looked after by Sheriff's Officers who worked at the court, while the judge and his staff travelled in their own vehicles, as did Brian Martin and Paul Rofe. Trevor and I drove a police car. Traffic policemen stopped traffic to help keep the group together when it was moving to view different locations at O'Connell Street and Ward Street, North Adelaide.

The jury took copies of the maps and plans with them to compare the documents with the actual locations. Brian Martin continued to point out various features at the different locations. We stood outside the Kelvin home and walked where Richard and his mate Boris walked on the evening Richard disappeared. We travelled to von Einem's Paradise home, stopped and went inside. We drove past the

Alcorn's property at Lower Hermitage where Thora von Einem stayed with her cousin on weekends before moving onto the airstrip where Richard was found. It is one thing to present photographs and drawings to a jury but if they can see the actual locations mentioned during the trial then the jury's understanding is much greater. The viewing of various locations doesn't happen in every trial, however, as the Sheriff's officers have to arrange security and transport and often police have to be present to stop traffic. Obviously, it's time consuming and costly.

At von Einem's home I showed the judge, prosecution and defence the ledge behind the mirror in von Einem's bedroom. Interestingly, the bedroom cupboards had been moved around in the bedroom and were against opposite walls. Perhaps von Einem or his defence team were trying to trip us up so that we would give confusing evidence in front of the jury. If the defence could show that we were uncertain about the location of cupboards in the bedroom, then they could cast doubt on the rest of our evidence. The jury followed afterwards because there was insufficient room for everyone in the room at one time. A sheriff's officer pointed out the ledge to the jury.

After the drive to various sites and addresses, Brian Martin introduced the first of the next thirty-five witnesses to the court. When he needed a break, Paul Rofe introduced new witnesses.

The second and third witnesses in the trial were Rob and Betteanne Kelvin. They provided two corner pieces to the jigsaw of evidence that was about to unfold. Both of them talked about their son. Rob Kelvin was first. He took the stand and gave positive evidence about his son, just as you would expect, but he didn't paint the picture that he was perfect. Brian Martin didn't ask the direct question about whether or not their son was 'normal'. Brian just asked his questions and the answers from Rob and Betteanne showed Richard was a normal fifteen-year-old.

'Yes, he was having trouble at school.'

'He had trouble with spelling and numbers and some students at Adelaide High School had picked on him. He was asked to repeat a year, which didn't help his self-esteem.'

'The learning difficulties encouraged them to place him at an alternative school — Marbury in the Adelaide Hills. He was much happier.'

'He smoked.' Rob Kelvin didn't like it but Betteanne smoked and she was less demanding.

'Yes, he had tried alcohol but he wasn't a drinker.'

Rob stressed that Richard never hitchhiked or accepted rides from strangers and he didn't like to be out and about at night. Betteanne Kelvin told the jury how she would meet him at the bus stop in Melbourne Street after school cadets at Hampstead Army Barracks in the northern suburbs on Friday nights. Richard wanted her to meet him because he didn't want to walk home in the dark.

His mate, Karl 'Boris' Brooks, who was Richard's last friend to see him, told a story to the court which reinforced what Rob and Betteanne were saying. Boris said that on the Sunday night Richard disappeared, he started to walk toward the bus stop near the Womens and Childrens Hospital on King William Road. However, Richard didn't want to go that way because it was dark and they had to cross some parklands. Richard wanted to go to the bus stop in O'Connell Street, North Adelaide instead. That is the reason why they went to the O'Connell Street bus stop.

The evidence of these witnesses powerfully indicated that Richard was not going to get into a car with a stranger.

Brian Martin also knew that he had to show that Richard was against homosexuality. Von Einem, in his alibi, was saying that Richard had gone with him voluntarily. He was suggesting Richard had homosexual tendencies and Brian wanted to show this was not the case. He asked Rob Kelvin about his son's views on homosexuality. Rob told the court that his son didn't like homosexuals and if he wanted to stir someone he would call them a 'poofter'. He used the word in a derogatory way.

Rob and Betteanne both told the court that Richard always had a girlfriend and Betteanne said he was so serious about his current one that Richard talked to his mother about getting engaged when they were nineteen. Richard's girlfriend, the girl he was supposed to have rung as soon as he got home from the bus stop, gave similar evidence about his views on homosexuality.

In my mind, however, Richard wearing the dog collar presented a problem for Brian Martin. If Richard was 'normal', why was he wearing a dog collar around his neck? Brian Martin asked his father about it.

'Did Richard have a dog collar with him when he left?'

'Yes.'

'Where was it at the time he left?'

'He put it around his neck.'

'You have a dog?'

'Yes.'

'Had he [Richard] ever worn the dog collar before?'

'No.'

'Were the boys messing around with it before they left?'

'Richard was the sort of boy who ... he was a boy who liked to play around. After cadets, for instance, he would march for us in the lounge room; he would march up and down and send everything up, like a comic. He was a comic and I just took him, putting the collar around his neck, as just one of his tricks, just being silly.'

Brian Martin took this point further with Boris.

'Had one of you been fiddling with the dog collar at Richard's home?' Brian said.

'Yes, he was fiddling with it when he was on the phone.'

'What did he do with it?'

'Put it around his neck.'

'Did he speak to you about it?'

'He thought he was Joe Cool.'

'Did he ask you what you thought of it?'

'Yes.'

'What did you say?'

' "You look ridiculous".'

'Did he wear it down the street?'

'Yes.'

'Did it seem to fit or was it tight?'

'It just fit him perfectly.'

'Did you see him take it off?'

'Yes.'

'When was that?'

'At the bus stop.'

'What did he do with it?'

'He was trying to put it around his knuckles.'

All of this evidence — from his parents, his best mate and another guy who saw him at the bus stop, reiterated that Richard was happy on that evening. He was not worried about things. His girlfriend said that he was okay on the telephone immediately before he left for the bus stop. He was a normal boy of fifteen. He was due home for dinner and was going to watch a movie with his parents that evening.

As the days went by, witnesses presented evidence about finding drugs in Richard's body and the visit to von Einem's home on 28 July 1983 when the drugs, including Mandrax, were found. Harry Harding from the Forensic Science Centre told the court that the hairs found inside Richard's underpants were identical to von Einem's. Sandra Young gave evidence about the fibres that Des Phillips found on Richard's clothing matching von Einem's passageway carpet, bedroom carpet and bedspread. Geoffrey Robinson, senior scientific officer in the Home Office in England, came to Australia to support Sandra's evidence and he gave additional damning evidence.

Brian Martin put von Einem's alibi to the scientist and asked about fibre transfer and 'the persistence of fibres' — the ability of fibres to stick to another material.

'The bedspread was of medium shedability on the top or upper side, the bedroom carpet was of low shedability, the hall-lounge carpet was of high shedability and I think I have already told you the Toyota car seat was of medium shedability. You have said that the factual situation I put to you was not a likely situation for the fibres found. Can it be considered a possible explanation for the fibres found?'

'Possible did you say?'

'Possible.'

'I would say impossible.'

This was a sensational statement. An eminent overseas scientist was saying that von Einem's explanation about Richard being in his house was impossible. He was saying von Einem was a liar.

Brian Martin continued.

'Just on that. In the United Kingdom do you have a practice or a cut-off period at which no fibre identification is attempted?'

'Yes, as a general rule of thumb one wouldn't examine clothing for contact fibres if the known contact was probably three days prior to the clothing being recovered.'

'What is the basis for doing that?'

'This is the figure of retention times recorded in the publications and one's personal experiences of recovering fibres.'

'That is, that it would be most unlikely to find fibres from a contact more than three days after the contact?'

'Yes, assuming the clothing had been worn normally during a period of three days it would get extremely unlikely to find any remaining fibres.'

Von Einem said that he picked up Richard on 5 June 1983, took him home and then dropped him in the city on the same day and didn't see him again. This meant that the fibres from his home and cardigan transferred to Richard on the Sunday night he went missing.

Geoffrey Robinson was saying that when Richard was found, eight weeks later, he should have had no or very few of the fibres from von Einem's environment on his clothing. This is what we found with fibres from Richard's home environment. There were only two fibres from his home left on his clothes. The same principle should have applied to the fibres from von Einem and his home. After eight weeks, there shouldn't have been that many fibres on Richard's clothing. What the international expert was saying was that contact with Richard was within three days of him being dumped — von Einem was with him at about the time he was murdered! The case against von Einem was getting stronger and stronger.

Also, there were no fibres from the maroon seats of the Toyota, which von Einem said he was driving that Sunday night. The seats in the Toyota had characteristics which indicated 'medium shedability'. That finding indicated that Richard Kelvin wasn't in the Toyota as von Einem said. That made it more likely he was in another car — possibly von Einem's Falcon sedan, which he sold a week after Richard was dumped.

Von Einem could have remained silent during the trial and Barry Jennings would have argued to the jury that they could not be sure that he was guilty of murder and should acquit him. He should have the benefit of the doubt. The law allowed this to happen. He had two other choices — to give sworn evidence from the witness box or to give an unsworn statement from the dock. The defence team thought he should present some explanation to counter the evidence that had been pieced together, but von Einem did not enter the witness box like Dr Millhouse did during his trial. Millhouse was in the witness box for three days giving sworn evidence and being grilled by the prosecutor. This time, Barry Jennings and Helena Jasinski elected for von Einem to give an unsworn statement from the dock so that he could not be questioned by Brian Martin.

Von Einem started reading his statement in his normal impassive way of speaking and acting. There was not one nervous mannerism.

'Ladies and gentlemen of the jury, I am not guilty of the murder of Richard Kelvin. I am thirty-eight years of age. I am single and, as I told the police last year, I am a homosexual. Up until my arrest I lived with my mother at ... Paradise. We moved there in late April 1983. Before that we lived for five years at ... Campbelltown.

'I worked for eighteen years at Pipeline Supplies of Australia at South Road, Regency Park as an office accountant.

'In 1982 I bought a Ford Falcon, registration number SXK–257, from Pipeline Supplies and sold it to Mr Bondarenko on Saturday, 16 July 1983. The registration of that vehicle expired on the 13th of July 1983. I sold that car because I did not need two cars and I wanted some money for my overseas trip.

'In or about Christmas 1981, before I bought the car, the muffler was replaced at premises on the corner of Main North Road and Grand Junction Road near Gepps Cross. After that time it had a normal exhaust. There was rust in the boot from a leaky esky and window seal. I painted the boot with epoxy resin to cover the rust and prevent it from spreading. I did that on a Saturday afternoon, either the 2nd or the 9th of July 1983. I am not sure which.

'The silver Toyota Corona was my other car. I was using that in June and July of last year. It, too, had a normal exhaust.'

Von Einem was explaining that he painted his boot because it was rusted and he wanted to sell it, not to hide any evidence. Also, he was saying that both of his vehicles had normal exhausts and was suggesting that the noisy car that was used to abduct Richard Kelvin was not one of his cars.

'On Saturday, 4th of June 1983, I had a garage sale at ... Street. My mother stayed that night at the Alcorn's house at Houghton. I was going to go out that night but did not because I began to feel ill. Later that night I locked myself out of the house and had to go up to Houghton to get door keys from my mother. I think it was about 10 p.m. I then came home and went to bed.

'On Sunday 5th June 1983, I went to the Railway Museum at Mile End with my nephew, Robert, in the afternoon. I was wearing my old brown cardigan because at the Railway Museum I was climbing all over engines and carriages. Robert and I went back to my place and Robert left.

'I then decided to go to O'Connell Street, North Adelaide to buy some fish and chips or a hamburger. I realise there are fish and chip shops closer to my home, but I fairly often used to go to O'Connell Street to get takeaway food.'

Earlier in the trial Brian Martin had the owners of five fish and chip shops situated between von Einem's home and North Adelaide give evidence to say whether or not their shops were open that fateful Sunday night. Brian was showing that von Einem was on the prowl that night, not just out buying fish and chips. Now von Einem was answering this evidence.

'I was driving the Toyota along O'Connell Street in a southerly direction but did not see a car park. I decided to drive around the block and turned left into what I now know was Boulton Street. I was driving along Boulton Street in a northerly direction. I was drinking a can of beer. At the time it was on the seat between my legs. When I was at about the junction of what I now know to be Marian and Boulton Street[s], a youth whom I now know to be Richard Kelvin ran in front of my car from Marian Street. I had to brake to avoid him. He was running. I wound my window down and he came over to the driver's side. He rested his arms on the roof, as I demonstrated to Detective Kipling on my interview on the 1st March this year and as you have seen him demonstrate to this court.

'I have heard Detective Kipling's evidence of the interview he had with me on 1st March this year. In that interview I did my best to tell Detective Kipling truthfully what I could remember of what happened between Richard Kelvin and I on the night of Sunday, 5 June last year. What I told him is what happened that night. There is nothing else of importance that I can remember now. I told Detective Kipling the truth and I ask you to accept what I told him as part of my statement to you.

'The last I saw of Richard Kelvin was when I dropped him off opposite the Royal Adelaide Hospital on that Sunday night.

I do not know anything about what happened to Richard Kelvin after that. At no other time was he at … Street.

'After I dropped Richard Kelvin off I returned home. I was going to pick up my mother but did not feel well enough to do so. Later I drove to my sister Carlien's to ask her to pick Mum up from the Alcorn's but I thought it was too late. So I rang up the Alcorn's house to say that I would not be up that night but would pick Mum up the next morning. I went back home and went to bed.

'The next morning, Monday 6th June 1983, I had a head cold and a sore throat. I was not well enough to go to work. My sister came around at about 9.30 a.m. and then went to pick up Mum. My mother came home later that morning and she and I stayed home the rest of the day until I went to Dr Cowan's surgery, but there seemed to be nobody there so I came home.

'Later that night I went to Dennis St Dennis to get my hair done. His cousin and mother were there. I told them I had a wog. Dennis was going on holidays and it was the only time he could do my hair.

'On Tuesday 7 June, I was feeling worse and my mother made an appointment for me at her clinic and I saw Dr Munro, as you have heard. He examined me and told me I had what was going around. He prescribed Amoxil, which I got from the chemist on the way home. He also gave me a sickness certificate for a week. My mother was home during that week and I slept a fair bit. Apart from taking my mother shopping at Target one afternoon, I did not go out at all later that week. Lynn Pratt from work came over on Thursday night with my pay. I was sick in bed when she came.

'The next weekend was a long weekend. I do not remember doing anything on the Saturday but on the Sunday night I went out as I told the police. On the Monday night some friends from the Harp Society came to our place. I went back to work on Tuesday, 14 June and worked there every workday until I went overseas on 11 August 1983.

'In the period from Tuesday, 14 June to Sunday, 10 July 1983, I do not specifically remember what I did most nights or on weekends. My mother was at home at nights and as far as I can remember at weekends too. My mother does not drive a car and if she went out at night in that period it would have been with me. I do recall that in the June/July period I worked back a fair bit as Mr Martin, my boss, said.

'Three nights that I do specifically remember now are: Tuesday, 21 June, when my mother and I went to a dinner party at a member of the Harp Society's house; Wednesday, 6 July, when I went to a Harp Society meeting; and Sunday, 10 July, when my mother and I went to a birthday party for a relative, Mrs Gladys Amoy.

'I slept in as usual on the Sunday morning and we arrived at the Amoy's some time late in the afternoon. We stayed there until about 10.30 p.m. or so. We took a lady by the name of Mabel Gough to her home and arrived home at about 11 p.m. I went to bed and did not go out again that night. I went to work the next day.'

It was interesting that everything that von Einem told about related to family and the Harp Society. Obviously, he didn't want to talk about any of his other friends — the businessman, the transvestites, the transsexuals and his young male friends.

'On Thursday, 28 July 1983 Detective Kipling questioned me about Richard Kelvin's disappearance and death. As you already know I did not tell Detective Kipling the truth about my involvement with Richard Kelvin on Sunday, 5 June. I did not want my mother to know that Richard Kelvin had been in her home. I realise now that I should have told the police the truth but as time passed I was frightened to tell anyone.

'As you have heard, the police found a number of different types of drugs at my home. You have also been told about medication that has been prescribed for me over the years. All the drugs found at my house were prescribed for me. Over the years I have required a lot of drugs for nerves, sleeplessness, anxiety and depression. The medication which I did not often use was kept on a ledge behind the mirror of my wardrobe. I have never been prescribed, nor have I ever used, Amytalobarbitone.

'On the night of Sunday, 5 June 1983, I did not give Richard Kelvin any drugs; I did not abduct Richard Kelvin or have any further contact with him after I dropped him off on North Terrace that Sunday night. I do not know what happened to him after that.

'I ask you to find me not guilty of murder.'

Von Einem's statement would have been written for him. He was intelligent enough to make up one of his own, but obviously Barry and Helena wanted to cover all of the points given by the witnesses. Von Einem's unsworn statement did not address the issue of hair and fibres. His defence team knew that would get him into trouble, so they left it alone.

Barry Jennings then asked Janet Amoy to take the stand. This was one of the defence team's last throws of the dice. Janet Amoy was the daughter of an elderly relative of Bevan's mother and she told of a birthday party for her mother that happened on 10 July 1983, the day Richard Kelvin was most likely dumped at the airstrip. She said that von Einem and his mother were at the birthday party from about 5.30 [p.m.] until 10.30 p.m. on that Sunday. If this was true, then at the most likely time Richard was dumped von Einem's presence was not possible.

Evidence was given by the dog man that he was walking his terriers on the airstrip on that Sunday afternoon. He walked his four dogs into the scrub where Richard was found and the body wasn't there at that time. Therefore, Richard had to be dumped on Sunday night, after von Einem had taken his mother and her friend home. This was a problem for our case. If Barry Jennings could raise doubt about any of our case we could be in trouble. Little things like that could bring us undone. The jury could imagine a person who worked a normal week dumping someone at night on a weekend. Sunday night would be nice and quiet but if von Einem was with relatives that night then jury members would start hesitating about any decision that they may make.

Brian Martin questioned Janet Amoy closely. Yes, she was sure that it was Sunday 10th July. Her mother's birthday was the next day but she wanted to have the celebration on the weekend. Also, her brother works on the Saturday in a hotel and she wanted him there. Yes, it was that weekend, there was no doubt in her mind. No, nobody suggested that she should come forward. She had been reading about the trial in the paper and remembered that the party was on that day.

How is Brian going to handle this? I thought. He hasn't knocked out her story.

Could we have made a mistake?

Barry Jennings called his next witness. It was Thora von Einem, Bevan's mother. She was seventy-four, grey and small, but she moved confidently and without support to the witness box. She opened her evidence by telling the court that she was a widow with two sons and a daughter. She had lived with her son Bevan von Einem at Paradise since April 1983. Before that, she lived with her son in a unit at Campbelltown for five years. Three days a week she was a volunteer at the North Eastern Community Hospital near her home.

Her evidence supported her son's story. She said that her son was home the weekend Richard went missing and was in bed with the 'flu most of the following week. He couldn't have been with Richard. However, under cross-examination, Brian Martin broke her story. Brian did a fantastic job but he had to be careful not to put the jury offside by attacking an elderly woman who appeared genuine and honest.

Brian reminded Mrs von Einem of a conversation she had with me when I spoke to her in August while her son was overseas in Europe between 11 August and 22 September 1983.

'Did you say to Mr O'Brien, "So Sunday he didn't go out. Saturday night you know he didn't feel well enough." Did you say that to Mr O'Brien?'

'I don't know about that, whether I did or not. I could have. I don't know. I'm sorry.'

'In fact, he did go out Saturday night, didn't he?'

'Yes.'

'He came up to Houghton.'

'Yes, that's right.'

'You don't know, do you, whether he went out on the Saturday or not?'

'No.'

Mrs von Einem also said in her statement to me that her son did not go out on the following weekend, but when Trevor interviewed him at the Adelaide Jail he said that he picked up two hitchhikers the following Sunday night. He was out and about picking up boys. Brian showed her to be a mother who would say things to support her son whether they were true or not yet he didn't show her to be an out and out liar. He just showed that she didn't really know what her son was up to.

Barry Jennings didn't re-examine Mrs von Einem. He appeared to accept that only more damage would be done. Mrs von Einem was Barry Jenning's last witness. He then presented the defence case. Barry was very clever in his summing up. He was cool and clinical. He stressed to the jury that his client did not have to prove his innocence. It was up to the prosecution to prove that von Einem murdered Richard Kelvin. Barry conceded that someone had killed Richard although the actual cause of death could not be proven. Barry Jennings may have made a mistake by conceding this. He did not have to do so. He could have stressed that it was up to the prosecution to prove murder — the intentional killing of a person. If the prosecution couldn't prove a cause of death, then the case is just that much weaker. Barry could have raised doubts in the minds of the jury about this point.

He stressed to the jury that although von Einem admitted he was a homosexual, this was no longer a crime in South Australia and being a homosexual did not make a person a murderer. He was appealing to the jury members' rationality, suggesting they should not be emotional with their decision. Barry Jennings also did not talk about the evidence of the fibres and hair in his summing up. He knew that it would remind the jury of this strong evidence against von Einem.

While Barry Jennings was cool and clinical, Brian Martin was far more emotive. He did not rant and rave, but the words were passionate and penetrating. During his address Brian did not refer directly to the damning evidence presented from the finding and examination of the hair and fibres but made the assumption that the jury accepted Richard was with von Einem. He talked about Richard's death.

'If the death resulted from an accident or if the death resulted in some way that was not murder why hasn't the accused told you? Why hasn't he stood up and said, "Look, it wasn't murder. I have done something wrong but it wasn't murder." Instead he's continued with his second false story. His first one goes way back to July. The only reason he changed that, you might think, was because the Crown could prove that [Richard Kelvin] had been in his house. He's continued with that.

'He cannot even get close to the truth for you because it's obvious that to do so would mean disclosing the names of his accomplices. Why wouldn't he be prepared to do that? Why wouldn't he tell you who they are? It is a fairly simple answer. He knows that if they are located they will further implicate him in the murder. If he's had nothing to do with the killing at all, why not say, "Yes, it was so-and-so and so-and-so, and go and see them." But he can't, because he knows that they probably know the truth of the matter, that they will, to use the colloquial expression, "put him in" for murder.'

Brian reminded the jury of the evidence of Richard's mother. This was a smart move. Recalling the evidence of Betteanne Kelvin balanced the more recent evidence of Thora von Einem, who said her son was home most of the first week Richard was missing.

' "Mum, I'm in love with Brigitta and I think we'll get married and have lots of kids."

'That, ladies and gentlemen, is the young man that this accused says just wandered up to the car, arms on the roof: "Can I have a beer?" Hopped in, "Let's go for a drive, let's go to your house. Forget about ringing [his girlfriend]. Forget about seeing the movie with Mum and Dad; don't worry about the fact that Mum and Dad are going to go around the bend because I'm not home." I could use a lot stronger word than nonsense to describe the story. If I did I would probably get into trouble.'

Brian asked rhetorical questions for the jury to ponder:

Why did von Einem drive in the opposite direction to North Adelaide when he was due to go and pick up his mother at Houghton?

Why didn't von Einem pick up his mother on the Sunday night?

Why was he travelling south along O'Connell Street when he saw Richard Kelvin? If he had just come in to town from home he would have been travelling north along O'Connell Street.

Why carry an esky in his boot when he drinks in moderation?

Why did he pick up Richard Kelvin?

Why did he take him home?

If he went to North Adelaide to buy fish and chips, why didn't he do that even after he picked up Richard Kelvin?

Why couldn't he call for a taxi from Paradise and let Richard Kelvin take a taxi from von Einem's home?

Why leave Richard in North Terrace and not take him to within fifty metres of home and let him walk home?

Why didn't he come forward earlier?

He argued that von Einem's story was lies, and answered the evidence of Janet Amoy, which placed von Einem at the family birthday party between 5.30 p.m. and 10.30 p.m. on the Sunday Richard's body was placed at the airstrip. He suggested that von Einem could have dumped Richard in the early hours of Monday morning after getting up very early to go to work.

Brian stressed that von Einem was involved in the beginning of the abduction — he admitted picking up Richard. He was involved at the end of the abduction and murder because the fibres and hair proved it. Finally, the drugs showed von Einem was involved between those times. It was a great address to the jury that eased many of our concerns.

Justice White had the final say and his views about the case were critical. The judge explained to the jury that matters of law are his domain and that the jury were obliged to follow his directions in this area. He also stressed that facts and inferences from the evidence and the demeanour of the witnesses were up to the jury to accept or reject. He reminded the jury that von Einem could not be criticised for giving an unsworn statement. He had the right to do that and he reminded the jury that von Einem had had the choice to speak up or remain silent.

Justice White said that the case depended on circumstantial evidence and that it was up to the prosecution to prove the case beyond reasonable doubt. He stressed that regardless of what was speculated on in the media there was no evidence to link the Richard Kelvin matter with any other murder. He wanted to make sure that the jury's verdict was not clouded by media reports about the other boys.

The jury retired to consider their verdict at 12.25 p.m. on 2 November 1984. They returned at 3.51 p.m. to ask the judge about what constitutes murder. This was a worry. They had the opportunity to bring in the alternative verdict of manslaughter but Brian Martin addressed only for murder. He said to the jury that it was murder not manslaughter but he knew that the judge would address this point with the jury. Justice White did this.

I wonder if they are going to find him not guilty of murder but guilty of manslaughter, I pondered. *Or could they possibly give him the benefit of the doubt and find him not guilty?*

At 7.51 p.m., shortly after the jury were fed in jury room seven, they returned to the courtroom.

'Have you reached a verdict?' The clerk of court asked the foreman.

'We have.'

'Do you find the accused guilty or not guilty of murder?'

'Guilty.'

Cheering and clapping broke out amongst the 100 people that had filled the public gallery. I have never heard or seen anything like it. In the 1980s, people sitting in the court just did not make any noise. They did not yell out obscenities or make comments to the defendant when the verdict was announced as happens quite regularly now. This was the first time I ever heard that sort of group emotion in a court. The courtroom presented an amazing scene. Initially, it was one of happiness and then relief that it was all over.

Bevan Spencer von Einem showed no emotion.

Trevor and I left the courtroom after Justice White said von Einem was to remain in custody for sentencing and he was returned to the cells in the basement of the building.

We walked out of the courtroom and wrapped our arms around one another and slapped each other on the back. We then turned to the other members of the team who were present to hear the verdict and shook their hands and slapped them on their backs.

Chapter 13

Additional Charges

Bevan Spencer von Einem was automatically sentenced to life imprisonment for the murder of Richard Kelvin but it was the non-parole period that was important. The non-parole period determined the amount of time that he had to spend in jail before being released, and it was up to Justice White to fix that period. He summed up his feelings:

'I deal with your case solely upon what has been proved in this court. Whatever may be the public or police suspicions so widely and so recently published alleging suspicion of some connection of this case with other cases, I must, and I do, fix this non-parole period solely on the basis of the facts proved beyond reasonable doubt in this case.

'The horrendous nature of this crime, involving, as it did, a long period of imprisonment and ill-treatment prior to murder, has added a new dimension to the kinds of murder committed in the State, with which the community has to live . . .

'You do not show remorse. You do not admit guilt. You showed yourself to be cool and violent at the time of abduction, inventive and resourceful during imprisonment of the youth, ready to resort to lies and false alibis after discovery of the body, and you are unrepentant at the moment.

'I fix a non-parole period of twenty-four years.'

The Attorney-General appealed straight away against lack of severity of von Einem's term of imprisonment. Twenty-four years imprisonment meant that he could be out of jail in sixteen years if one third of the non-parole period was taken off for good behaviour while in prison. They argued that twenty-four years imprisonment was too light and Brian Martin on behalf of the Attorney-General asked the Court of Criminal Appeal to increase the sentence.

On 29 March 1985, Chief Justice King and Justices Jacobs and Olsson handed down the results of the appeal. They said in their findings:

'The present crime . . . indicates such depravity of character on the part of the perpetrator that his absence of previous convictions loses its significance. The abduction, captivity, sedation, homosexual abuse and murder of the boy did not occur on impulse and could only have been perpetrated by a person or persons of grossly depraved character.'

The Supreme Court increased von Einem's non-parole period to thirty-six years' imprisonment, the highest imposed on anyone in South Australia to that time. With remission, von Einem would be out of prison during 2009. He would be sixty-two years of age.

After the end of the appeal, Barry Jennings had moved on but Helena Jasinski was still involved with the von Einem defence. David Peek now came on board as the barrister for von Einem. The new defence team appealed to the Court of Criminal Appeal. They complained about the evidence which related to Richard being against homosexuality and not having homosexual inclinations. Peek challenged the relevance of this evidence and the way it was introduced into the trial.

Also, references to von Einem's homosexuality were given during his trial. The defence team submitted that this evidence showed von Einem to be of bad character and would have caused the jury to be biased against him. They also argued that Justice White's address to the jury did not summarise the defence case. He ignored the evidence of von Einem's relatives, which indicated that von Einem could not have dumped Richard at the time suggested — on Sunday, 10 July 1983. Finally, they argued that there was a miscarriage of justice caused by the way in which Justice White summed up the case. They argued that the judge invited the jury to speculate rather than to consider the evidence.

The Appeal Court rejected most of the defence arguments saying that von Einem's crime revolved around homosexuality and abuse, and Richard's views about homosexuality helped the jury consider whether or not von Einem's alibi was likely to be true or not. Richard would not have behaved the way von Einem said he did if he was against homosexuality. Also, the Appeal Court pointed out that just because von Einem was an admitted homosexual, it did not mean that he committed homosexual crimes. Von Einem's crime was proven by other evidence and not by his admissions about his sexuality.

The Appeal Court agreed that Justice White's address to the jury would have been better if the evidence disputing the time of dumping was mentioned. However, the appeal judges thought that, overall, Justice White put the defence case to the jury 'fully and fairly' and that his discussion of theories and explanations about Richard's murder were quite proper.

Justice Olsson as a member of the Appeal Court said:

'The plain fact of the matter is that it is difficult to see how, upon a dispassionate review of the evidence, a reasonable jury could have brought in a verdict other than that which it did. The whole of the circumstances established by the Crown pointed unerringly to the guilt of the accused and I consider that no substantial miscarriage of justice occurred.'

We were pleased after all this time that an independent review of the evidence and court proceedings found we had a strong case that was handled well by Brian Martin and Paul Rofe. Finally, when discussing von Einem's non-parole term, the appeal judge said:

'As a sole murder, the accused's crime has established new depth of depravity in South Australia's history ... Indeed I would go so far as to say that the circumstances of this crime are such that they must come very close to the borderline of constituting a special reason for declining to fix any non-parole period. The community has every right to expect that its judges will do their best to ensure that a person who has been party to and/or capable of conduct so abhorrent as that revealed by the evidence and who has shown no remorse whatsoever will not be released until it appears clear that he will no longer constitute a danger to others.'

Trevor and I, as a team, investigated one more case after the arrest of von Einem for the murder of Richard Kelvin. The case involved the vicious murder of an elderly couple at Monteith, near Murray Bridge, about 120 kilometres south east of Adelaide. We arrested one of the two young men, who was convicted of killing the couple and Doug Kokegei, who worked on another team, arrested the other one in Melbourne. Shortly after that case I left to do a bosses' course and became what the police and the military call a commissioned officer.

Trevor remained at Major Crime. He was promoted and made a sergeant, and, after I left, he worked with Malcolm Howells and they continued to work on the Family Murders as well as other killings. They monitored the appeals and continued to investigate leads as they were received at Major Crime.

The investigation went quiet for the next four years. In March 1988, the State Coroner, Kevin Ahern, who has now retired, was about to inquire into the death of Mark Langley. He had already conducted inquests into the deaths of Alan Barnes and Peter Stogneff. Tom Ferguson, one of the bosses in the detective branch, sent a letter to the coroner requesting that he inquire into the deaths of all the boys. Tom requested a joint investigation because the police held the view that there were similarities between the deaths. Kevin Ahern agreed to do so. He reopened the inquests into

Alan Barnes and Peter Stogneff and included them in his new inquiry. This inquest did not include the Richard Kelvin murder because it had been the subject of a successful criminal trial but the Coroner did not ignore the circumstances of Richard's abduction and murder.

Pathologists, Ross James and Colin Manock, gave evidence at the inquest. Ross James was the pathologist who examined Alan Barnes and Neil Muir and he gave evidence to the Coroner about the anal injuries to the two boys.

'If I can ask you a very general question with respect to the anal injury,' Kevin Ahern asked, 'in your opinion is there any similarity between the injuries which you observed with Muir and Barnes?'

'There is in the sense that the anus was ruptured. The nature of the anal injury was that it was torn and cut. Some blunt object had stretched the anus to the point where it was torn,' Ross James said in evidence.

This, officially, provided the first link between the murders of Alan Barnes and Neil Muir. The counsel assisting the Coroner also asked about the cutting up of Neil Muir and Peter Stogneff.

'Yes, in this case the body [Stogneff] in effect has been cut into approximately three equal pieces. The cuts were at the level of the lower backbone above the pelvis, in this instant at the level of the third lumbar vertebra. Secondly, each lower thigh was sawn to above the level of the knees. The difference from, for instance, Muir, is that there is no evidence that the head had been cut off from the trunk.'

'But the other cuts in location first of all were virtually in the same position as those of Muir?'

'Yes.'

Ross James was providing a similarity between the murders of Neil Muir and Peter Stogneff, and he gave additional evidence to say that the anal injuries of Alan Barnes, Neil Muir and Mark Langley were similar. Some form of blunt instrument, such as a bottle, caused the tearing of the anus. Here was a respected expert stating there was a link between the murders of three of the boys and, if the cutting up of Neil Muir and Peter Stogneff was similar, then, indirectly, he was linking all five murders.

Colin Manock, the other pathologist, also gave evidence to the Coroner. He talked about the cut to Mark Langley's abdomen that was roughly stitched. He said that this wound would have given access to the anal canal, allowing the removal of any object which may have been forced into the anus. Colin was suggesting that an object could have been inserted into Mark's anus and then removed by rough surgery. Trevor and I had always speculated that Mark's murderer was forcing something into his anus and possibly lost it in Mark's anal tract. We believed he was cut open to retrieve it. Colin Manock was giving evidence that this may have happened.

Trevor Kipling also gave evidence at the Coroner's inquest. He had been working on the murders for nearly seven years and he gave very clear evidence about them when he answered a question from the counsel assisting the Coroner.

'It may be obvious from what I have said to you, leaving Kelvin aside for a moment, [but] did the police form a view as to whether the deaths of Barnes, Muir and Stogneff and Langley were connected?'

'Yes.'

Trevor had not wavered in his view that the same people were involved with four of the murders. His reasons included the manner in which the young men were murdered, the way their bodies were redressed and dumped and the drug link. He also supported the evidence of Ross James referring to the similarities of the cutting up of Muir and Stogneff.

Coroner Ahern then commented that there were similarities in the deaths of Alan Barnes, Neil Muir, Mark Langley and Richard Kelvin.

'In each case, there was the presence of a substantial anal injury, washing of the body after death, redressing the body in the cases of Langley and Barnes and the dumping of all bodies in a locality other than where the murder occurred. In the cases of Langley, Barnes and Kelvin, it was likely there was a period of detention prior to the death and also the presence of certain drugs ... In relation to the deaths of Barnes, Langley and Muir, it is my own personal view that more than one person was probably involved in the original abduction and subsequent murder. It would be difficult, in my view, for one person alone to abduct persons of the stature particularly of Barnes and Langley and, perhaps to a lesser extent, Muir. The same comment may apply in the case of Kelvin deceased.'

To help revisit and understand the murders, the table on the following page provides an overview of the facts.

The Coroner presented his findings on Thursday, 24 March 1988 about the manner in which the boys had been picked up as well as findings in relation to the murders of Alan Barnes, Neil Muir, Peter Stogneff and Mark Langley.

	Barnes	Muir	Stogneff	Langley	Kelvin
Last seen	Sunday	Sunday	Thursday	Sunday	Sunday
When dumped	Saturday	Monday	N/K	Monday	Sunday
When found	Sunday	Tuesday	Wednesday	Monday	Sunday
Date last seen	17 June 1979	26 August 1979	27 August 1981	28 February 1982	5 June 1983
Date dumped	23 June 1979	27 August 1979	N/K	1 March 1982	10 July 1983
Date found	24 June 1979	28 August 1979	23 June 1982	8 March 1982	24 July 1983
Period of detention	Yes	No	N/K	Yes	Yes
More than 1 person	Yes	Yes	N/K	Yes	Yes
Drugs	Noctec, alcohol	Barbiturates	N/K	Mandrax	Mandrax, Noctec, Valium, Amytal
Injuries	Anal, eye injury, broken bones	Anal, head injury, dissected	Dissected	Anal, incision to abdomen	Anal, head injury, brusing
Redressed	Yes	No	N/K	Yes	Yes
Vehicle used	Yes	Yes	Yes	Yes	Yes
Location where dumped	North-east	North-west	North	East	North-east
Property missing	No	Yes	Yes	Yes	No
Food taken just before death	Yes	N/K	N/K	At party	Yes

'It is apparent from the evidence of Detective Sergeant Kipling that a number of methods were adopted. According to him the main methods were a feigned vehicle breakdown, a lure in the car, in which there would be a reasonably good-looking female or transvestite who would then lure the innocent hitchhiker or pedestrian into the vehicle. On the other hand, it could be a straight hitchhiker situation where the hitchhiker was approached, invited into the car, given a drink which, on many occasions, was laced with some form of drug. This was known of course as a Mickey Finn. A common drug used for this purpose was Noctec, or chloral hydrate. Certain other drugs were also used on occasions including that known as Mandrax. The effect of these drugs with the combination of alcohol rendered the victim sleepy or indeed unconscious. The victim would then be taken to certain premises where various indecencies would be performed upon the body of the victim, including anal intercourse and no doubt other lurid practices.

'I have, in fact, perused a number of statements from victims who fortunately survived the ordeal. Statements given by these people have been checked and rechecked and there is no doubt that their account of what happened are substantially true and certainly not fanciful.'

Kevin Ahern called for the reward for giving information about the murders to be increased. It had started at $5000 when Richard had first disappeared and risen to $15,000. The amount of money offered by the Government quickly jumped to $100,000 by the time von Einem was arrested, and the reward was eventually for information about all the boys' murders. Later, in March 1988, it was raised to a new high of $250,000. The Government was accepting that there was a link between them. Community concern had increased markedly, and the

Government reacted to that. Now, Kevin Ahern asked for the reward to be increased again and it was raised to the extraordinary sum of $500,000 in September 1989.

Police interviewed many people over the years following the conviction of von Einem. They found more women who were with von Einem when he picked up and drugged boys and they again confirmed what we knew about his activities. However, parts of the investigation led nowhere, were inconclusive, and took an increasing amount of time and effort. Even when I was still involved, we had organised a line-up using a witness who thought she had seen Peter Stogneff at a Tea Tree Plaza coffee shop on the day he disappeared. The line-up included von Einem but the witness could not pick him as the person with the boy. Also, we didn't know whether or not the boy with the man was actually Stogneff. This possible sighting happened on a Wednesday, which was different to the rest of our findings; von Einem usually went on the prowl on weekends and his work records did not show him to be away from Pipeline Supplies on that day. However, we felt that the records wouldn't be entirely accurate as von Einem was in a position to manipulate them. So, even though Trevor was convinced that all the murders were linked, there were some differences and these really complicated the investigation.

Things changed when Detective Kent McFarlane went to Sydney on 5 September 1989 to speak to B again. He gave another statement, which convinced Prosecutor Brian Martin to offer him immunity against prosecution if he gave evidence against von Einem. The immunity related to offences that he committed in relation to abusing boys but did not apply if he was involved in the actual murders. This was arranged and again it was time for Trevor to act.

On Friday, 15 September 1989, Trevor went to Yatala Prison and spoke with von Einem for a short time. This time Trevor taped the conversation, which was only three pages long when it was transcribed.

'Bevan, how are you?'

He did not reply so Trevor introduced Malcolm Howells and Lyn Dunstan, the two detectives who were with him.

'What has happened is that we have got direct evidence now that implicates you in the murder of Alan Barnes.'

'That is impossible.'

'OK. The situation is you don't have to answer any further questions at this time, do you understand that?'

'Yes, I understand that.'

A short time later, Trevor said: '... so the situation is you are being arrested for the murder of Alan Barnes and shortly you will be conveyed to the Adelaide Watch House where you will be formally charged, do you understand that?'

'I understand that.'

'Is there anything you want to tell me about it?'

'I have nothing to tell you.'

Trevor Kipling again returned to the jail on 10 November 1989 in the presence of Mark Griffin, von Einem's new solicitor. This time, Trevor told the prisoner that he was going to be charged with another murder. He was going to be charged with the murder of Mark Langley when he next appeared in court for that of Alan Barnes.

The committal hearing to determine whether or not

there was enough evidence to send von Einem to trial for the two new counts of murder started on 5 March 1990 before David Gurry, an experienced magistrate whose grey hair and black-rimmed glasses suited his profession. The committal started nearly eleven years after the murder of Alan Barnes and eight years after the murder of Mark Langley. Trevor Kipling certainly had been persistent with his investigation. Other detectives would have given it away a long time ago.

Von Einem was asked to stand in the dock and the charges against him were read out.

'Bevan Spencer von Einem, you are charged that between the 16th June 1979 and the 25th June 1979 at Adelaide or another place you murdered Alan Barnes. How do you plead?'

'Not guilty.'

'Bevan Spencer von Einem, you are also charged that between the 26th February 1982 and 9th March 1982 at Adelaide or another place you murdered Mark Andrew Langley. How do you plead?'

'Not guilty.'

The wording of the charges indicated a weakness in the case. After all these years, we still could not show where the boys were actually killed. We knew that Richard Kelvin was at von Einem's Paradise home at about the time he was killed but he could have been taken there just before or just after he was killed. From the scientific evidence, I certainly believed that Richard was killed there.

Many places were checked over the years as being possible locations where the boys had been killed, but too much time had passed before the houses were checked for blood, fingerprints and cutting instruments, such as a saw and a knife. We had located the homes of most of the women where von Einem took boys who he had picked up. However, four years had passed between the times Alan Barnes and Richard Kelvin went missing and another six years passed before these new charges were laid and members of von Einem's clan, had moved homes at least once.

From the beginning of the committal, Mark Griffin and Marie Shaw, von Einem's new defence counsel, argued that there would be an abuse of justice if von Einem was committed to stand trial. There had been too much publicity about the murders and the possibility of von Einem's involvement for him to receive a fair trial.

This time Brian Martin was assisted by Tom Birchell, and Brian argued that the case against von Einem with respect to Alan Barnes revolved around von Einem picking up hitchhikers. There were von Einem's denials about knowing the boys, but B said von Einem was with Alan Barnes immediately before he was killed. The Mark Langley case relied on evidence that von Einem also denied knowing Mark Langley on 25 March 1982, when he was interviewed at the Adelaide Jail. He admitted driving around on that night, including being near the River Torrens during the early hours when Mark went missing. Circumstantial evidence showed also that his death was similar to Richard Kelvin's.

When Detective John Anderson spoke to von Einem about the murder of Mark Langley, von Einem said that he was out and about that night. He said that he was drinking at home and left for a drive at about 11 p.m. He took the back streets to miss random breath stations. He drove through back streets to the Hackney Hotel, which is next to the Hackney Bridge, which crosses the River Torrens. He drove to North Adelaide and drove down Melbourne Street and up the hill to O'Connell Street, North Adelaide and bought some fish and chips — just as he said he intended to do when he grabbed Richard Kelvin. This man was a creature of compulsion and habit. He said he drove to Pipeline Supplies of Australia and checked the security lights before travelling along Port Road and Hindley Street. He went to the Mars Bar at 1.30 a.m. before leaving at 3.00 a.m. to travel home by the back streets of Stepney — exactly the way Mark Langley would have been trying to go home.

As I read this statement and the statements of the females who picked up boys for von Einem, all the theories and practices recorded about the stalking phase of serial killers rang true. These actions reminded me of someone moving out at night going for a hunt — looking for prey.

Different women gave evidence about von Einem picking up boys. One of the 'females' who von Einem used as bait gave evidence. She met von Einem at Number One beat in 1972, when she was a man. She changed her sex ten years later, in 1982. She was also a druggie who had a problem with Mandrax when it was commonly available. After Mandrax, she was addicted to heroin. She told the court about Mandrax and the picking up of boys, which she did about ten times with von Einem.

'They were called "randy mandies" and they would often go around a pub — [the] best way to start an orgy was for that sort of thing to happen.

'... it was never a planning thing. It would just happen. Like, I could be getting a lift — and it would usually be weekends. Weekends were mainly the times he went out. And, I mean, it wasn't like he'd ring me up or I'd ring him up and we'd say "Let's go out and pick up hitchhikers" or anything like that. It would be if I was getting a lift with him, he might just divert and start doing that.'

Yes, I thought. Just like Miller with Christopher Worrell picking up girls who later ended up the Truro victims. Miller said that the picking up wasn't planned. They didn't have to plan it because it was a natural thing both of them did. This was no different.

'What time of the night did that occur, if there was a particular time?' Brian Martin asked.

'Usually late at night and sometimes it could have been from ...' she paused '... I could have been over at a friend's place and wanting a lift home if I wasn't going to sleep there.'

'Did the defendant ever say anything to you about the type of hitchhikers that he liked?'

'He didn't say the type that he liked; he just ... the type that he liked were young, sort of rough-looking people.'

'Was there any word in the gay scene for that type of person or any expression that covered them?'

'Probably "rough trade".'

'Is that just based on their appearance, that expression rough trade?'

'Yes.'

'Are you talking about persons who gave the appearance of being homosexuals or persons whose appearance was heterosexual or either?'

'Persons who gave the appearance of being heterosexual.'

'What age group were the hitchhikers that you either attempted to pick up or on the couple of occasions you've told us you were successful?'

'From any age up until about twenty-five, I suppose.'

The oldest of the murdered boys was twenty-five, I thought back to myself. Neil Muir was that age. The picking up of heterosexual hitchhikers provided a form of conquest.

'What sort of age at the bottom end?'

'At the bottom end, the only person that — as I said yesterday, one time when we stopped and spoke, and they obviously knew each other — he looked about fifteen, but I don't know what age he was. He looked very young. I don't know if that was because he was very small or what. He just seemed to look very young.'

I recalled the deviate, B, in his statement to me about von Einem saying that one of the boys did not even have pubic hair. Von Einem is quite a man.

Other witnesses gave evidence about von Einem picking up hitchhikers and drugging them but B was the main witness for the prosecution. He also spoke about von Einem picking up hitchhikers, but he also gave more damning evidence. B said that he met von Einem at Number One beat and von Einem had Alan Barnes with him. He was present when von Einem rang the businessman.

'Do you want to come and do some surgery on this guy?' von Einem said on the phone.

'They were going to make a video out of what happened and they were going to kill Barnes,' B said to the court.

Also, a witness had come forward after all of these years — one that we didn't even know about, and he said that he was with Alan Barnes during the last week of his life. He was with Alan twice when he met von Einem in the Gateway Hotel on North Terrace, Adelaide. Von Einem was talking about the boys going to a party where there would be girls and drugs — it was all so familiar. Now, we had evidence of von Einem actually being with Alan Barnes.

Later, he gave more evidence, which was even more sensational. B was responding to the questions of Brian Martin.

'Had he ever said anything to you about being involved in the deaths of other persons, be they adults or children?' Martin asked.

'Yes.'

'When had he said something to you about that?'

'A few weeks before the Barnes incident. He told me that he'd picked up three children and that he connected them all together and that one of them died. And he told me that he dumped the bodies at Moana or Myponga. I can't remember which he said. It was either Moana or Myponga. He also told me that he'd picked up two children at the football and killed them.'

'Two children at the football and killed them?'

'Yes.'

'Did he mention names?'

'No. He did mention the Beaumont children regarding the first incident, but he didn't mention anything of the second incident.'

This was sensational! Now we had B saying that von Einem admitted killing the Beaumont children, and the Ratcliffe and Gordon girls. The trouble was that B was a self-confessed druggie and liar. He had previous convictions for possessing marijuana, theft and loitering. He had by now been spoken to or interviewed by the police five times and each time his story changed. He added extra detail each time.

His sister gave evidence at the committal and she told the sensational tale that her brother had seen her at her home at Gawler one weekend and he was hyped up and said that he had just seen a murder. He said that he had seen someone murdered and thrown over a bridge. He would have been talking about the murder of Alan Barnes. Did that mean he was involved with that murder? If he was there, he had to be, but he always denied being involved. He always said that he bowed out when the really nasty things were about to happen. B's sister said that she didn't believe him when he told this story. She said that he was always telling lies. When I spoke to him in 1983 for six hours, he said that he didn't know anything about the Barnes matter except for what he had already told police, and that he wasn't involved in the murder of Alan Barnes.

Von Einem was committed to stand trial in June 1990 but the defence team weren't happy about the evidence that had been admitted by Magistrate David Gurry at the committal.

They were arguing that B's evidence about the Beaumonts, and the Ratcliffe and Gordon children was an abuse of process and the publicity it received prevented von Einem from receiving a fair trial. They filed a notice of motion and a supporting affidavit for the trial not to proceed. They argued that there would be a miscarriage of justice.

Justice Kevin Duggan was appointed to review their application. He commenced on 19 June and gave his findings on Monday, 17 December 1990, deciding that the matter should proceed to trial. However, he had a list of concerns about the evidence, which included: the alleged confession of von Einem about the murder of the Beaumont children, and the Ratcliffe and Gordon girls; the pencil incident; the evidence of the hitchhikers and associated evidence; the chain of evidence of the drugs in relation to the Barnes' case; the similar fact evidence involving Richard Kelvin's murder; the similar fact evidence involving the Mark Langley murder; and the evidence of B.

Justice Duggan was signalling problems with the prosecution case and Brian Martin was worried. He was relying on the hitchhikers and the story of Richard Kelvin's death to show that von Einem picked up and killed Alan Barnes. If the jury accepted that von Einem killed Alan, then Brian would argue that the jury could then conclude he also killed Mark Langley.

Coincidentally, Kevin Duggan was appointed the trial judge. This was appropriate because he now intimately knew the case and the evidence which would be presented. When the trial started on Wednesday, 19 December 1990, the judge intimated at the very beginning he would let B give evidence but would hear defence objections to his story as he went along. However, he excluded the evidence of the murder of Richard Kelvin and the evidence of the hitchhikers and von Einem's associates. The similar fact evidence of the associates and the hitchhikers showed that von Einem picked up and drugged boys but it didn't prove he killed them — the evidence was just not similar enough for the law. Brian Martin's prosecution case just fell apart.

On Friday, 21 December 1990, Brian Martin received instructions from the Attorney-General not to proceed with the Mark Langley murder charge against von Einem. Brian was going to try to fight on with the remaining murder charge. He still had von Einem lying about knowing Alan Barnes and witnesses would say Alan was with von Einem the day before he was murdered but, without the evidence of the hitchhikers, he knew he was still in trouble with his case. And on 1 February 1991, over eleven years after the murder of Alan Barnes — the first of the murders, the final murder charge against von Einem was pulled. The Attorney-General advised prosecutor Brian Martin to enter a *nolle prosequi* — the charge was not to proceed, although this does not mean he can't be charged again if more evidence is found.

Unfortunately, the drama didn't stop there. Von Einem and his defence team have used legal ploys without success to have his case reopened. In September 1996, about fifty boxes of police files were seized after an application by defence solicitor, Mark Griffin, for the investigation to be reviewed. They were alleging that von Einem was under police surveillance at the time Richard Kelvin was being held captive and therefore he couldn't have been involved. This was soon discounted because surveillance didn't start until after we first interviewed von Einem on 28 July 1983, after Richard's body was found. This aspect was reviewed by an independent legal expert from Victoria and he found no basis for the claim. The Liberal Attorney-General Trevor Griffin (no relation to the defence solicitor of the same name) accepted the review's findings and the application to reopen the case failed.

By 22 December 1997, a new defence solicitor was in on the case. Michael Abbott, Queen's Counsel, the high-profile defence lawyer, petitioned the Governor, Sir Eric Neale, for mercy for von Einem. He argued that there was new evidence to support von Einem's alibi. A witness said that he saw Richard Kelvin in Rundle Mall after Sunday, 5 June 1983 when Richard was abducted. His statement, if true, meant that von Einem's alibi was right after all and the Governor should accept a plea for mercy. The difficulty was that the man was an admitted bisexual and he knew von Einem. Also, his description of Richard was inaccurate when he said that he was wearing earrings in both ears and one in his nose. Richard didn't wear earrings in his nose and the post-mortem showed no holes to indicate that he ever had worn them there. The Governor refused the petition on advice from the then Attorney-General Griffin.

Through all these legal machinations, von Einem continued to protest his innocence, repeating his alibi about taking Richard Kelvin home to show him his harp, and denying that he killed the boy.

His claims of innocence were ironic in a way. Everything he said simply knocked over any remaining doubts of his guilt the people of the city of Adelaide may still have had.

Even though the world had been involved in a revolution of social customs, religious beliefs, and sexual politics — and Adelaide was not immune to any of it — there was still a sense in the minds of much of the community that this was 'little old Adelaide'. Life was safe here, not like in the bigger cities of Sydney and Melbourne. Adelaide was not the kind of place where this sort of thing went on.

Von Einem put paid to that very smartly. He was the latest in a long line of killers who had stalked the city's streets and public places and snatched away its youngsters. He was obviously not responsible for all of the serial killings that had occurred over the decades — but he certainly was one of our weirdest murderers.

Chapter 14

The Rumours

Tolerance and freedom were the buzzwords of the 1960s and 1970s as established cultural and social patterns were changing everywhere. People were experimenting with drugs and sex; normal conservative couples were wife swapping and homosexuals were coming out, seeking to be considered as normal members of the community. Sexual preferences were a private matter, just like politics or social attitudes.

In an extraordinary leap from conservative backwater to liberal (small 'l') frontline, South Australia found itself forging a reputation for being a reformist state. Liquor licensing and gaming laws were eventually relaxed, and, in time, homosexuality between consenting adults in private was legalised. It was the era of a brave and charismatic premier, Don Dunstan, whose government was, in his own words, 'democratic socialist'. He practised liberalism in its broadest sense and set about promoting changes right across every spectrum of society, including in the political and legal fraternities.

Don Dunstan wrote about this in his own book, *Felicia*. After his Labor Party came to office he was made Attorney-General, and when it came time to appoint a Chief Justice, after the retirement of Sir Mellis Napier from the position, Don Dunstan decided it was time to break with tradition. He nominated a notable law lecturer at the University of Adelaide, Dr John Bray, rather than selecting one of the existing judges to be appointed to the senior position. Don Dunstan wrote in his book that Dr Bray was from the establishment but lived a bohemian existence. What he didn't say was that Bray was thought to be a homosexual.

Don Dunstan relates in his book the story of the appointment of an excellent person to a senior office within the State. Dunstan recommended to Cabinet a person for the job, but the Premier of the day, Frank Walsh, told Dunstan that this man was not a fit person for the job. The Premier had received advice from the then Commissioner of Police, John McKinna. The police commissioner told Dunstan that the nominee was a homosexual and that homosexuality was still a crime in the State. Don Dunstan demanded to know the evidence that raised such an allegation. McKinna mentioned the rumour and innuendo about the man. Dunstan wrote: 'I flew into a temper and demanded to know how he dared to traduce a citizen and endeavour to interfere with Cabinet appointments on such a basis.'

Three days later, the Commissioner produced patrol logs from police that mentioned three occasions on which police were suspicious about his behaviour but there was no evidence of his homosexuality. Firstly, the person was seen sitting in a car late at night talking to a man in the Adelaide parklands. It was not clear whether or not it was near one of the beats. Secondly, patrol officers stopped outside the person's house to question a passer-by and saw him get up with another man from behind the garden wall of his house and walk inside. The third report mentioned how police had been despatched to a part of his house, which had been rented separately. Some transvestites were present but Don Dunstan wrote that the man under suspicion was not there at the time.

'I looked at the Commissioner with astonishment and fury. I indicated my disgust in round terms — the matters in the patrol reports indicated no action not capable of perfectly innocent explanation,' Don Dunstan wrote. Later, Cabinet accepted his nominee.

These were strange words from a person who was a professional politician and who would have understood the power of rumour and innuendo. I think Don Dunstan protested too strongly in his book, because by the end of his career it was accepted that Dunstan was a homosexual and may have favoured homosexuals in some of his appointments. The changing world and the activities of Don Dunstan in the 1960s and 1970s with his appointment of a reputed homosexual to a senior position within government began all kinds of rumours about prominent people. It also set the scene for stories of prominent people within Adelaide's society being involved in the boys' murders and rumours about the existence of a high-level 'Family' began to spread throughout the city.

Trevor continued to investigate the murders and, as a separate initiative, commenced Project Egret in 1989, which gained intelligence on paedophilia and led to a task force of police, called Operation Torpedo, investigating this crime in South Australia. This task force was interested in the so-called 'Family' but the initiative occurred as a result of rising national and international concerns about child abuse. About eighty people were jailed for offences relating to child abuse but they were not, in reality, connected with the Family.

Members of the legal fraternity were interviewed as part of police investigations and rumours that a legal person, Peter Liddy, was a member of the Family were untrue. The Attorney-General in 1989, Chris Sumner, went public and said categorically that the rumours were wrong. Police agreed with this view. And years later, a magistrate would come under notice for having sex with minors, but he, too, was not a member of the Family.

The denials of the Attorney-General did not quell the rumours, which were spreading through Adelaide like wildfires. In fact, the denials seem to fuel the fire. Many people became aware for the first time of members of the legal fraternity being homosexuals. The rumours intensified, so that the Family now reputedly included not only members of the legal profession, but also politicians and members of Adelaide's elite.

These rumours were all wrong. They were urban myths.

And they weren't helped by the unfortunate coincidence of the surname of the former Attorney-General in the

Liberal Government, Robin Millhouse. He had the same surname as Doctor Peter Millhouse, who had been charged with the murder of Neil Muir. The public appeared to think that there was a relationship between the two of them. Also, Adelaideans seemed to have forgotten that the doctor was acquitted of the murder charge. The rumours were simply built on false foundations.

Obviously, investigations need to cover all possibilities to ensure that strangers, not acquaintances, abducted Richard Kelvin. Trevor Kipling had made sure that all the people coming in contact with Richard were checked out. One of those people was Rob and Betteanne's gardener. I briefly spoke with him in the front garden of the Kelvin home early in the investigation. A single man, he was tall, tanned and ruggedly handsome. He couldn't offer any information about Richard's disappearance in the days after he went missing but several weeks later I received a letter from him. The letter came through the normal postal system into the internal mail system of the police. The letter was thrown into my wire basket on my desk. I didn't know who it was from when I opened the envelope and started reading. The further I read the letter, the more my mouth dropped open. It appeared to be a love letter!

'What is a nice young man like you doing the job that you do. You are too nice for that type of work ...' were some of the words used.

When my composure came back, I had a bit of a laugh about it and showed it to Trevor. We kept quiet about it as we didn't want any rumours starting about Richard and his family's connections. We were satisfied that he wasn't involved but if there were rumours about the gardener then more resources would have to be diverted in that direction. Also, it may have started rumours about Richard being a homosexual. We knew he wasn't and we didn't need any rumours to complicate the investigation.

The rumour concerning Richard probably started after the media publicised that he was wearing a dog collar when he went missing, but it was the reporting of von Einem's alibi that fueled it. Von Einem suggested that Richard had homosexual tendencies with his story that he had taken him home to play his harp. Anyone not following the case closely would have read about the alibi, and perhaps some newspaper readers or radio listeners could have thought that von Einem's version was true. Those who knew the whole story knew it to be calculating lies in an attempt to beat the murder charge. Those in the court and those people in the jury heard how the prosecution completely discredited his alibi. There was nothing to suggest that Richard was a homosexual — on the contrary, all the pointers were facing the opposite direction. Richard Kelvin did not have homosexual tendencies. He was interested in women and he took the dog collar from his neck when he was told that it made him look silly.

Von Einem continues to protest his innocence and still says that he let Richard go after he picked him up. He says that someone else picked him up after he let him go. He doesn't try to explain why he had hidden drugs in his bedroom. He doesn't explain about those drugs which were found in

Richard's body and in other boys whom he picked up and abused. He doesn't give an answer to the scientific evidence, which shows Richard Kelvin at his home at about the time he was murdered, not five weeks earlier as von Einem claimed. Von Einem does not give an explanation for his lies other than to say he didn't want to upset his mother, who already knew he was gay. So, why should he have to hide the fact that he brought Richard home from his mother, if he did nothing wrong? He doesn't say anything because his answers will implicate him and his associates even more. The evidence showed his guilt and yet von Einem continues to tell his same story time and time again, working on the belief that if you say it long and loud enough someone will believe you. However, as in most crimes, the victims are not the only ones directly involved. On the other side of the ledger, families hurt forever. Betteanne Kelvin expressed her grief on 7 February 1991, one week after the last charge against von Einem was dropped. She wrote a letter to *The Advertiser* newspaper.

> *When your child is murdered everything you have ever believed in is destroyed. Your belief in a happy future is taken. Your belief in your child's right to grow and have a happy life with children of his or her own [is] ripped away ... The only tangible thing you can hang on to is the belief that in the society we live in, justice will prevail.*

Chapter 15

The Family

The sub-title, referring as it does to 'The Family Murders', was an appropriate one in the broadest sense. Von Einem had a natural family as we all do. His mother gave evidence during the trial and supported her son. He also has a brother and sister who live in Adelaide. As mothers do, his does not truly believe the guilt of her son. She knew her son was a homosexual but she didn't know the side of her son that went on the prowl on weekends. Deep down she must have had concerns lingering in her mind. She must have believed something was not quite right. The odd hours he kept would have sent those signals to her. Also, other members of his family, on reflection, might have wondered if something was not right. Like the night von Einem took a boy to Lower Hermitage where the Alcorns lived — the home where Thora von Einem stayed regularly. Von Einem bogged his car on the property and Ken Alcorn found both of them and allowed them to stay the night. The car was freed the next day and von Einem left. Nothing happened on the property but what was von Einem doing with the boy?

Von Einem also had close friends. Like most of us, he only had a few really close friends but von Einem also had many associates. They were part of his 'extended' family; not a blood family but some of them were linked through the abuse of boys and the spilling of young blood.

Obviously, there were others close to von Einem at the time who have not spoken out or have only told half the story. They were von Einem's 'extended family' of deviates and were probably involved intimately with the murder.

There was no doubt that von Einem murdered Richard Kelvin. The jury thought so and the Court of Criminal Appeal thought so as well. The facts of the Kelvin case and the details from the other murders show that he would have to be a very strong suspect to be one of the killers of Alan Barnes and Mark Langley as well.

I believe that von Einem was involved with the murders of Alan Barnes and Mark Langley. The drugs, anal injuries and circumstances surrounding their deaths all point to von Einem and the Family. Alan Barnes, like Richard Kelvin, was most likely killed at von Einem's Paradise home and in the same way as Richard Kelvin. We know Richard was in von Einem's home at about the time of his death and then he was dumped in the Adelaide Hills to the north-east of the city. Alan Barnes was dumped in the same area.

The Family would also have to be strong suspects in the

murders of Neil Muir and Peter Stogneff but we can be less positive about this than with the other three boys. Peter Stogneff was the third boy to be killed and, because the killers had no luck disposing of the first two, both Alan Barnes and Neil Muir being discovered in their watery graves, their killers most likely simply started dumping the boys on the side of the road.

When Trevor Kipling first said that the same people killed all the boys it made sense. The murders were all so similar but then, after we found out about von Einem, he followed up with a statement which stunned me.

'You know, I think that he has done the lot.'

'Yes, I know that,' I said.

'Yes, but von Einem has done the Beaumonts, and Ratcliffe and Gordon as well.'

'Come on ... bullshit. How can that be? We're looking at boys being murdered — the others were girls.'

'There was a young muscular man seen at Glenelg with the Beaumonts — he had blond hair. Von Einem has been white-haired since he was eighteen and he would have been twenty when the Beaumonts went missing. Also, a man was seen with some kids on the banks of the River Torrens when Ratcliffe and Gordon went missing. Why couldn't the same person be responsible?'

I didn't believe Trevor at first. Why would a person move from picking up girls and murdering them to picking up and killing boys? Intuitively, it didn't make sense. However, as I reflected on this theory, I thought that it could just be possible. The youngest of the Beaumont children was a boy. Also, von Einem could have been testing his sexuality at twenty years of age; maybe there was an interest in girls but, if the theory was true, more than likely the children were just young people who he could abuse — the sex didn't really matter. Von Einem was just interested in playing around with bodies.

We had B saying in evidence that von Einem admitted to him that he had picked up and killed the children. Either von Einem was big-noting or he was bragging about what he actually had done. Trevor's insights into the case were truly amazing and our superdeviate had to be considered as a suspect for the Beaumont, and Ratcliffe and Gordon murders all those years ago. Just how good the theory is, I don't know.

Any success solving these bizarre murders is unlikely to come from physical evidence linking someone to them. Trevor had police divers search the Myponga reservoir for the Beaumont children. At that time, people could drive over the dam wall and it would have been easy to drop the Beaumont children over the side, just as Alan Barnes was dropped over the bridge at the South Para Reservoir. The divers failed to find any bodies but it would be unusual to find anything in water after such a long period of time, especially against a dam wall, which would have silt building up against it. Other locations, like the Alberton house and two other places used to take boys to, have been demolished — the passing of the years has reduced any likelihood of any physical evidence remaining there. Any new evidence is more likely to come from members of the Family who, except for the businessman, have moved on or away. They will carry their guilt with them for the rest of their lives. However, one member does not seem to feel any guilt or remorse — that person is Bevan Spencer von Einem.

Obviously, as with all investigations, mistakes were made. When I spoke with Trevor about it years later he felt that we should have made more effort to target the minor players who were involved picking up boys with von Einem. More pressure could have been placed on the drag queens and transvestites who assisted von Einem with places to take the boys. We knew they helped von Einem. They did it for the drugs he supplied them with, and the sex with the boys. Did they assist more than they admitted? The dumping of the bodies indicated this was possible. Now it is probably too late to put any more pressure on them. The element of surprise has been well and truly lost.

Another mistake was made by the uniform police about the time of the disappearance of Alan Barnes. B and von Einem picked up two hitchhikers and they were driving around town getting them drunk and off their faces on rollies. While they were doing this they needed to go to the toilet so von Einem stopped his brown Falcon sedan in a side street that came off Hindley Street. B and one of the boys were taking a piss, another was being sick from the booze and the drugs, and a police car came along. The uniformed officers asked what they were doing — obvious as it was. Von Einem had made the mistake of driving the wrong direction in a one-way street and the police car had followed them. The police asked them their names but didn't book them. Sure enough, they weren't serious offences — von Einem could have been booked for driving the wrong way in the street and B could have been reported for urinating in a public place. But more effective police might have taken greater notice of the two boys in the back of the car and a few questions about them should have caused them to smell a rat. However, the police accepted the comments of von Einem, and then later those two boys were abused, and narrowly escaped the fate of the others.

We tried for a long time to locate a record of von Einem being stopped by the police, but von Einem and B were not recorded in any of the police logs. No record of the boys' names was found. Even though some boys who had been abused by von Einem were found and did give statements, many were not and it may be they were the ones who had key evidence as well.

The Family, not 'the family' of rumour and innuendo, but the real one, still exists. One senior member is in jail. The other senior member is still in Adelaide, both with his business and with his homosexuality. However, time has moved on and the brothers in crime have separated. No longer do they have 'family meetings'. No longer do they hunt in packs. But will we ever close the book on the unsolved killings? Hopefully, the reward of $500,000, which is still available for information leading to the conviction of anyone responsible for the murders, will tempt someone to come forward with information, and the words of Coroner Ahern will prove to be prophetic.

'Finally, acting on the assumption that more than one person was involved in at least some of the murders [it] should be remembered by those responsible, that enquiries are ongoing. It can only be hoped that in due course and time the persons may be brought to justice for the horrific crimes in which they participated.'

I again met one of von Einem's young associates about two years after I interviewed him in 1983.

I was driving home after working afternoon shift and guess who I saw hitchhiking? It was him for sure; he was walking along on Sir Edwin Smith Avenue, which veers away from King William Road immediately after the King William Street Bridge. He was trying to thumb a ride from passing cars.

What a coincidence, I thought. The River Torrens flowed under the bridge about fifty metres away. Here he was again so close to the river which was a focus of police investigations for so long.

I knew he lived in the northern suburbs of Adelaide not far from my home. I stopped the police car. He ran to the front passenger door and opened it.

'How about a lift?' he asked before I could say anything.

I thought about it very briefly. People aren't allowed to ride in police cars without permission — at least there needed to be a proper reason.

Why not? You never know what he might say, I thought. Stranger things have happened during investigations. One word, one action, can change the direction of an investigation.

'Jump in,' I said.

I drove off heading north and we started talking.

'Do you remember me?' I asked.

'It's you,' he said looking over to the driver's seat. His face was untroubled.

I knew straight away that nothing was going to happen during the drive to his home. He was not concerned at all about getting into a police car. He simply wanted a ride home and he was getting it, just like the many he had cadged in his teenage years. It didn't matter that his chaffeur was the police officer who had interrogated him about a cruel abduction and vicious murder. He seemed to have no fear. Or no memory that remained alive from those days. An innocent person would perhaps show some concern that the police had got it wrong and that the new meeting might lead to charges wrongly being laid against him. A guilty person might show some hint in his eyes or his throat with a swallow to moisten a dry mouth. Not this guy. He showed no remorse or guilt. There was no emotion. It was just a ride home.

He was still young but experienced in the use of drugs and homosexual sex. I felt he had stopped worrying about the rights or wrongs of his previous life. He appeared to have accepted his life as it was and appeared unconcerned about the direction it was taking. His face showed no emotion — he reminded me of a young von Einem.

The rest of the drive was uneventful. He told me that he had spent some time in Queensland and now he had returned to Adelaide. The words that passed between us could be best described as small talk. What remained unsaid ... well, who knows? Twenty minutes later I dropped him off near his home and he walked into the darkness of the Adelaide night.

www.ingramcontent.com/pod-product-compliance
Ingram Content Group Australia Pty Ltd
76 Discovery Rd, Dandenong South VIC 3175, AU
AUHW020722180626
428720AU00024B/65

9 780732 269135